PORTUGUESE PICTURE DICTIONARY COLORING BOOK

Over 1500 Portuguese Words and Phrases for Creative & Visual Learners of All Ages

Color and Learn

Free Book Reveals The 6-Step Blueprint That Took Students **From Language Learners To Fluent In 3 Months**

- **6 Unbelievable Hacks** that will accelerate your learning curve
- **Mind Training:** Why memorizing vocabulary is easy
- **One Hack to Rule Them All:** This secret nugget will blow you away...

Head over to **LingoMastery.com/hacks** and claim your free book now!

CONTENTS

Introduction..1

Basics of the Portuguese Language 2

Emoções (Emotions) 15

A Família (The Family) 17

Relacionamentos (Relationships) 19

Valores (Values) 21

O Corpo Humano (The Human Body)... 23

Dentro do Corpo Humano (Inside the Human Body) 25

Animais de Estimação (Pets) 27

O Zoológico (The Zoo)... 29

Pássaros (Birds)... 31

QUIZ #1 33

Répteis e Anfíbios (Reptiles and Amphibians) 35

Insetos e Aracnídeos (Insects and Arachnids)................................... 37

Mamíferos I (Mammals I)... 39

Mamíferos II (Mammals II) 41

Peixes e Moluscos (Fish and Mollusks) 43

Roupas I (Clothing I)... 45

Roupas II (Clothing II).. 47

O Clima (The Weather) 49

As Estações – Primavera (The Seasons – Spring).............................. 51

As Estações – Verão (The Seasons – Summer) 53

QUIZ #2 55

As Estações – Outono (The Seasons – Fall/Autumn)....................... 57

As Estações – Inverno (The Seasons – Winter) 59

As Horas (Time)..61

A Casa (The House)...63

Itens de Cozinha (Kitchen Items)..65

Itens do Quarto (Bedroom Items)..67

Itens do Banheiro (Bathroom Items)...69

Itens da Sala de Estar (Living Room Items)..71

Itens da Sala de Jantar (Dining Room Items)...73

QUIZ #3...75

O Jardim/Quintal (The Garden/The Backyard)...77

A Área de Serviço (The Cleaning Room)...79

A Escola/A Universidade (The School/The University).................................81

O Escritório (The Office)...83

Profissões (Professions/Occupations)..85

Meios de Transporte (Means of Transport)...87

Paisagens (Landscapes)...89

Esportes I (Sports I)..91

Esportes II (Sports II)...93

Dia de Natal (Christmas Day)...95

QUIZ #4...97

Instrumentos Musicais (Musical Instruments)...99

Frutas (Fruits)...101

Vegetais (Vegetables)..103

Tecnologia (Technology)...105

Ciências (Science)...107

Astronomia (Astronomy)...109

Geografia (Geography)...111

O Hospital (The Hospital)...113

A Fazenda (The Farm)..115

QUIZ #5...117

Comida (Food)..119

Pratos (Dishes)..121

Frutos do Mar (Seafood) 123

Formas (Shapes) 125

O Supermercado (The Supermarket) 127

Mídia (Media) 129

A Feira/O Parque de Diversão (The Fair/The Amusement Park) 131

Eventos da Vida (Life Events) 133

Adjetivos I (Adjectives I) 135

QUIZ #6 137

Adjetivos II (Adjectives II) 139

Advérbios (Adverbs) 141

Direções (Directions) 143

O Restaurante (The Restaurant) 145

O Shopping (The Mall) 147

Verbos I (Verbs I) 149

Verbos II (Verbs II) 151

Construção I (Construction I) 153

Construção II (Construction II) 155

QUIZ #7 157

Plantas e Árvores (Plants and Trees) 159

O Carnaval (The Carnival) 161

A Oficina (The Workshop) 163

O Mercado (The Grocery Store) 165

Viagem e Vida I (Travel and Living I) 167

Viagem e Vida II (Travel and Living II) 169

Brinquedos (Toys) 171

A Festa de Aniversário (The Birthday Party) 173

Opostos (Opposites) 175

QUIZ #8 177

Conclusão 179

Respostas 180

INTRODUCTION

The Brazilian Portuguese Picture Dictionary Coloring Book is a fun vocabulary-building tool with illustrations you can color while studying. It covers an immense range of topics that will help you learn everything related to the Portuguese language in daily subjects, from family members and animals to parts of the body and describing jobs.

This introduction is a guide to help you get started in Portuguese and polish your basic grammar, spelling, punctuation, and vocabulary skills. Good luck – and **most importantly, enjoy yourself!**

BASICS OF THE PORTUGUESE LANGUAGE

I.   Spelling and Pronunciation

a.   The Portuguese Alphabet – a Built-in Guide to Pronunciation.

Certain letters are pronounced differently in your native language and in Portuguese. Some letters may not even exist in your language. You must therefore learn to recognize these letters and pronounce them correctly.

A (*aah*)	H (*aahgah*)	O (*oh*)	V (*veah*)
B (*beah*)	I (*ee*)	P (*peah*)	W (*dublew*)
C (*seah*)	J (*zhota*)	Q (*keah*)	X (*sheez*)
D (*deah*)	K (*kah*)	R (*eh heah*)	Y (*eepslon*)
E (*eh*)	L (*ehllee*)	S (*ehcee*)	Z (*zeah*)
F (*ehfee*)	M (*eahmee*)	T (*teah*)	
G (*zhe*)	N (*eahnee*)	U (*ooh*)	

To improve your pronunciation, you must also learn to pronounce letter combinations such as "*ão*", "*nh*", "*ch*", "*al*"...

b. Pronunciation

The best way to achieve good Portuguese pronunciation is to listen, as often as you can, to movies or radio broadcasts. You will notice that Portuguese contains several sounds not used in English, which can only be learned by listening and imitating. Here is a quick guide on how to pronounce the most common letter combinations:

Vowels

<u>Short vowels</u>

A -> sounds like a*ah* -> as in *other*

Á -> sounds like a*ah* -> as in *acquire*

À -> sounds like a*ah* -> as in *amusement*

Ã -> sounds like *hum* -> as in *uncle*

Â -> sounds like uh -> as in *up*

E -> sounds like *eh* -> as in *heavy*

É -> sounds like *eh* -> as in *bet*

Ê -> sounds like *ih* -> as in *this*

I -> sounds like *ee* -> as in *hint*

Í -> sounds like *ee* -> as in *beach*

O -> sounds like *au* -> as in *clock*

Ó -> sounds like *au* -> as in *awe*

Ô -> sounds like *oe* -> as in *toe*

U -> sounds like *ooh* -> as in *moon*

Ú -> sounds like *ooh* -> as in *move*

<u>Vowel combinations</u>

AI -> sounds like the letter *i* -> as in *cry*

AL -> sounds like *ow* -> as in *house*

AM -> roughly sounds like o*un* -> as in *drown*

AN -> sounds like *un* -> as in *run*

AO -> sounds like *ow* -> as in *house*

AÕ -> roughly sounds like o*un* -> as in *crown*

AU -> sounds like *ow* -> as in *house*

EI -> sounds like the letter *a* -> as in *name*

EL -> sounds like *eo* -> as in *Romeo*

EM -> sounds like *am* -> as in *ambassador*

EN -> sounds like *an* -> as in *ant*

EU -> sounds like *eo* -> as in *Romeo*

IA -> sounds like *eah* -> as in *Georgia*

IE -> sounds like *yeah* -> as in *yes*

IL -> sounds like *ew* -> as in *few*

IM -> sounds like *eem* -> as in *imperative*

IN -> sounds like *in* -> as in *insecure*

IO -> sounds like *eoh* -> as in *yogurt*

IU -> sounds like *ew* -> as in *few*

OA -> sounds like *oah* -> as in *Noah*

OE -> sounds like *ue* -> as in *glue*

ÕE -> sounds like *oin* -> as in *coin*

OI -> roughly sounds like *oi* -> as in *noise*

OL -> sounds like *ol* -> as in *all*

ON -> sounds like o*n* -> as in *icon*

OM -> sounds like o*m* -> as in *from*

OU -> sounds like the letter *o* -> as in *no*

UA -> sounds like *wa* -> as in *wash*

UE -> sounds like *we* -> as in *went*

UI -> sounds like *wi* -> as in *wisdom*

Consonants

C -> sounds like *k* -> as in *cave*

C + I/E -> sounds like *ss* -> as in *cell*

CH -> sounds like *sh* -> as in *shell*

D at the end -> sounds like *t* -> as in *train*

G -> sounds like *guh* -> as in *gap*

G + I/E-> sounds like *zh*-> as in *leisure*

H + vowel -> is silent -> as in *hour*

LH -> sounds like *ll* -> as in *million*

NH -> sounds like *gn* -> as in *champagne*

R -> sounds like the letter *h* -> as in *house*

R before vowels, in the middle of a word -> roughly sounds like the letter *r* -> as in *rate*

S -> sounds like the letter *s* -> as in *sun*

S between vowels -> sounds like the letter *z* -> as in *these*

T before A, E, O, U -> sounds like a hard *t* -> as in *tea*

T in some cases before I -> sounds like *ch* -> as in *champion*

Grammar – Verbs and Tenses

I-   Glossary

Verb: A word that describes an <u>action</u>.

Tense: It tells you <u>when</u> an action happens/happened/will happen, etc.

Subject: It refers to <u>who</u> is doing the action. Verbs have different endings for each person.

Singular	eu	*I*
	tu, você	*you*
	ele, ela	*he/she/it*
Plural	nós	*we*
	vocês	*you*
	eles, elas	*they*

Ending: Usually represented by the last two letters in a word. It will tell you what tense you are in and what person you are using.

Stem/Root: The part of the verb that remains once the ending is removed, **or** the part used in the infinitive form.

Infinitive: The only form of the verb you will find in the dictionary. It usually ends in –AR, –ER, –IR.

Regular verbs: A verb that always follows standard patterns.

Irregular verbs: A verb that will either not follow a pattern or will have an irregular root.

Ajudar	To help
Eu ajudo	I help

5

Eu ajudei	I helped
Eu ajudei	I have helped

Irregular verbs: A verb that will **either** not follow a pattern **or** will have an irregular root.

FAZER	TO DO
Eu faço	*I do*
Tu / Você faz	*You (singular) do*
Ele / Ela faz	*He / She / It does*
Nós fazemos	*We do*
Vocês fazem	*You (plural) do*
Eles fazem	*They do*
SER / ESTAR	*TO BE*
Eu sou / estou	*I am*
Tu / Você é / está	*You (singular) are*
Ele / Ela é / está	*He / She / It is*
Nós somos / estamos	*We are*
Vocês são / estão	*You (plural) are*
Eles / Elas são / estão	*They are*

II-   The Present Tense

It tells you what happens as a general rule or what is happening at the time of speaking.

a) How to form it

Remove the ending used in the infinitive form, which is usually –AR, –ER, –IR. This will give you the stem. Then, add an -O in the case of I; an -A / -E / -I in the cases of you (singular), he, she, it; an -AMOS / -EMOS / -IMOS in the case of we; and an -AM / -EM in the cases of you (plural), they.

		Caminhar	To walk
Eu	+o	*Caminho*	*Walk*
Tu / Você	+a/e	*Caminha*	*Walk*
Ele / Ela	+a/e	*Caminha*	*Walks*
Nós	+amos / emos / imos	*Caminhamos*	*Walk*
Vocês	+am / em	*Caminham*	*Walk*
Eles / Elas	+am / em	*Caminham*	*Walk*

<u>Ex:</u> *Trabalhar* (to work) -> *trabalh-* -> *você trabalha* (you work)

Viver (to live) -> *Viv-* -> *Nós vivemos* (we live)

Insistir (to insist) -> *Insist-* -> *Eles insistem* (They insist)

ATTENTION:

- If the verb ends in –AR, you will use the suffixes +o; +a; +amos; +am.
- If the verb ends in –ER, you will use the suffixes +o; +e; +emos; +em.
- If the verb ends in –IR, you will use the suffixes +o; +e; +imos; +em.

b) Uses of the present tense

- To say what happens repeatedly (every year, every day, on Tuesdays).
- To say what is happening at the present time.
- To say what is happening in the immediate future.

- To say what has been happening for some time or since a particular time and is still happening.

III-   The Future Tense

It tells you what will happen.

a) How to form it

For the future tense, you should add a suffix to the infinitive form of the verb. Add an -EI in the case of -I; an -Á in the cases of you (singular), he, she, it; an -EMOS in the case of we; and an -ÃO in the cases of you (plural), they. Colloquially, people often use the verb IR (go) as an auxiliary verb followed by the infinitive form of the main verb.

Eu	*Infinitive + ei*	*Vou + infinitive*
Tu / Você	*Infinitive + á*	*Vai + infinitive*
Ele / Ela	*Infinitive + á*	*Vai+ infinitive*
Nós	*Infinitive + emos*	*Vamos + infinitive*
Vocês	*Infinitive + ão*	*Vão + infinitive*
Eles / Elas	*Infinitive +ão*	*Vão + infinitive*

Ex: *comer* (to eat) -> *Eu comerei* (I will eat)

   comer (to eat) -> *Eu vou comer* (I am going to eat)

ATTENTION:

In some cases, you should always use the SUFFIXES instead of IR:

- To sound more formal

b) Uses of the future tense

- To say what will happen.

IV-   The Conditional Tense

It tells you what would / may / might happen.

a) How to form it

Apply the same method used in the future tense, except now you should add the suffix -IA after the full infinitive.

Eu	*Infinitive + ia*
Tu / Você	*Infinitive + ia*
Ele / Ela	*Infinitive + ia*
Nós	*Infinitive + íamos*
Vocês	*Infinitive + iam*
Eles / Elas	*Infinitive + iam*

b) Uses of the conditional tense

- To say something hypothetical about a present or future situation.
- Often used in if/then statements.
- "Supposed-to-be" situations -> *Ela deveria vir às 15:00h.* (She was supposed to come at 3 o'clock.)
- To politely request something -> *Eu gostaria da massa, por favor.* (I would like the pasta, please.) Or to suggest something by asking "wouldn't it be better if…? -> *Não seria mais fácil se fizéssemos isso na internet?* (Wouldn't it be easier if we did this on the internet?).

V-   The Past Tense

It tells you what has happened in the past.

a) How to form it

In Portuguese, there are three different conjugations for regular verbs in the simple past, which depend on whether the verb ends in –AR, -ER, or IR.

1- Regular verbs

	Verb-AR	Verb-ER	Verb-IR
Eu	*Stem + ei*	*Stem + i*	*Stem + i*
Você	*Stem + ou*	*Stem + eu*	*Stem + iu*
Ele / Ela	*Stem + ou*	*Stem + eu*	*Stem + iu*
Nós	*Stem + amos*	*Stem + emos*	*Stem + imos*
Vocês	*Stem + aram*	*Stem + eram*	*Stem + iram*
Eles / Elas	*Stem + aram*	*Stem + eram*	*Stem + iram*

2- Irregular

There are many irregular verbs in Portuguese. Here is a list of the past tense (singular) of some of the most common verbs:

Infinitivo	*Eu*	*Você/Ele/Ela*
Dar	*Dei*	*Deu*
Deter	*Detive*	*Deteve*
Entreter	*Entretive*	*Entreteve*
Estar	*Estive*	*Esteve*
Instruir	*Instruí*	*Instruiu*
Intervir	*Intervim*	*Interveio*
Colorir	*Colori*	*Coloriu*
Obstruir	*Obstruí*	*Obstruiu*
Obter	*Obtive*	*Obteve*
Ouvir	*Ouvi*	*Ouviu*
Pedir	*Pedi*	*Pediu*
Ser	*Fui*	*Foi*

Infinitivo	*Eu*	*Você/Ele/Ela*
Ir	*Fui*	*Foi*
Ler	*Li*	*Leu*
Manter	*Mantive*	*Manteve*
Medir	*Medi*	*Mediu*
Mentir	*Menti*	*Mentiu*
Fazer	*Fiz*	*Fez*
Perder	*Perdi*	*Perdeu*
Poder	*Pude*	*Pôde*
Pôr	*Pus*	*Pôs*
Querer	*Quis*	*Quis*
Saber	*Soube*	*Soube*
Trazer	*Trouxe*	*Trouxe*

3- Uses of the Past tense

- To say what happened in the past.

VI-   The Present Perfect

In Portuguese, there is no difference between Present Perfect and Simple Past.

VII-   Word Order

Subject	Verb	Manner	Place	Time
Eu	*aprendi*	*com alegria*	*na escola*	*esta tarde*
I	have learned	with joy	at school	this afternoon

Key rules:

- The subject sometimes gets dropped in Portuguese.
  - *Está um lindo dia.* (It's a beautiful day.)
- After the subject and verb, add the direct object. After that, you can add the indirect object.
  - *Eu escrevo a carta com a caneta.* (I write the letter with the pen.)
- Most adjectives are placed after the noun they describe.
- Adverbs that modify a verb come after the verb in most cases.

VIII-   Pluralization

In Portuguese, the most common way to pluralize a noun is by adding -S.

General Rule:

a) How to form it

Singular	Plural
Porta (door)	Portas (doors)
Sofá (couch)	Sofás (couches)

ATTENTION:

- Replace the M with N. *A viagem* (the trip) -> *As viagens* (the trips).
- Replace the L with I. *O casal* (the couple) -> *Os casais* (the couples).

Exceptions

a) How to form it when the noun ends in R, S, or Z:

Singular	Plural
O prazer (the pleasure)	*Os prazeres* (the pleasures)
O mês (the month)	*Os meses* (the months)
O juiz (the judge)	*Os juízes* (the judges)

ATTENTION:

- In certain cases, when the noun already ends in S, you should not add another -S after the noun. As in *O ônibus* (the bus), *Os ônibus* (the buses).

IX- Vocabulary

Below you will find a short list of useful vocabulary to use in everyday life.

Portuguese	English
Segunda-feira	Monday
Terça-feira	Tuesday
Quarta-feira	Wednesday
Quinta-feira	Thursday
Sexta-feira	Friday
Sábado	Saturday
Domingo	Sunday
Oi	hello
Bom dia	good morning
Tchau	goodbye
Obrigada/o	thank you
Sim	yes
Não	no
Sanduíche	sandwich

Portuguese	English
Um	one
Dois	two
Três	three
Quatro	four
Cinco	five
Seis	six
Sete	seven
Oito	eight
Nove	nine
Dez	ten
Café da manhã	breakfast
Jantar	dinner
Nome	name
Idade	age
Velho	old
Por favor	please

13

X-   Final notes

Please note that this introduction is a brief overview of the Portuguese language. Portuguese is known for its complex grammar and many exceptions. This introduction will give you a good foundation to further develop your Portuguese language skills.

Genders are also touched upon lightly. The common way to change the gender of an adjective or noun is simply to replace "o" (masculine) with "a" (feminine). You will see examples in several chapters, where we have either written the full word in masculine and feminine or added "/a" at the end for your understanding. Pronunciation changes from "oo" to "ah" in this case.

Lastly, please be aware that you will find more details about the pronunciation of the Portuguese language as you go through the following sections.

EMOÇÕES (EMOTIONS)

1) **feliz** (happy)
feah-LEEZ

2) **triste** (sad)
TREEZ-ty

3) **animado/animada** (excited)
un-e-MAH-doo/dah

4) **bravo/brava** (angry)
BRAH-voo/vah

5) **surpreso/surpresa** (surprised)
sur-PREAH-zoo/zah

6) **preocupado/preocupada** (concerned)
preah-oo-koo-PAH-doo/dah

7) **com medo** (scared)
KOM MEAH-doo

8) **curioso/curiosa** (curious)
koo-ry-OE-zoo/zah

9) **entretido/entretida** (amused)
en-treah-TY-doo/dah

10) **confuso/confusa** (confused)
com-FOO-zoo/zah

11) **doente** (sick)
doe-EN-ty

12) **levado/levada** (naughty)
leah-VAH-doo/dah

13) **sério/séria** (serious)
SEH-ry-oo/ah

14) **focado/focada** (focused)
foh-KAH-doo/dah

15) **entediado/a** (bored)
en-teah-dy-AH-doo/dah

16) **sobrecarregado/a** (overwhelmed)
soh-breah-cah-heah-GAH-doo/dah

17) **apaixonado/a** (in love)
ah-pah-e-shoh-NAH-doo/dah

18) **envergonhado/a** (ashamed)
en-veahr-goe-GNAH-doo/dah

19) **ansioso/a** (anxious)
un-see-OE-zoo/zah

20) **nojento/a** (disgusting)
noe-ZHEN-too/tah

21) **ofendido/a** (offended)
oe-fan-DEE-doo/dah

22) **decepcionado/a** (disappointed)
dy-zah-pon-TAH-doo/dah

Ele está bravo com você.
He is angry with you.

Meus avós ainda estão muito apaixonados.
My grandparents are still very much in love.

A refeição de ontem me deixou doente.
Yesterday's meal made me sick.

A FAMÍLIA (THE FAMILY)

1) **avós** (grandparents)
   ah-VOHS

2) **avó** (grandmother)
   ah-VOH

3) **avô** (grandfather)
   ah-VOE

4) **tio** (uncle)
   TEW

5) **mãe** (mother)
   MUH-e

6) **pai** (father)
   PAH-e

7) **tia** (aunt)
   TEE-ah

8) **primo** (cousin, m.)
   PREE-moh

9) **irmão** (brother)
   eer-MUH-oo

10) **eu** (me)
    EH-OO

11) **esposo/esposa** (husband/wife)
    ez-POE-zoo / ez-POE-zah

12) **irmã** (sister)
    eer-MUH

13) **prima** (cousin, **f.**)
    PREE-mah

14) **sobrinho** (nephew)
    soh-BRI-gnoh

15) **filho** (son)
    FEE-llio

16) **filha** (daughter)
    FEE-lliah

17) **sobrinha** (niece)
    so-BRI-gnah

18) **neto** (grandson)
    NEH-toe

19) **neta** (granddaughter)
    NEH-tah

20) **sobrinho-neto/sobrinha-neta**
    (male/female second cousin)
    soh-BRI-gnoh NEAH-toe
    soh-BRI-gnoh NEAH-tah

- **Família do Conjugê (In-laws)
  – Parentes (Relatives)**

  Fah-MEE-llia doe KOM-zhoo-zheah

  – Pah-REN-teahz

21) **sogro** (father-in-law)
    SOE-groe

22) **sogra** (mother-in-law)
    SOH-grah

23) **cunhado** (brother-in-law)
    koo-GNAH-doo

24) **cunhada** (sister-in-law)
    koo-GNAH-dah

25) **nora** (daughter-in-law)
    NOH-rah

26) **genro** (son-in-law)
    ZHEN-hoe

27) **tio** (uncle-in-law)
    TEW

28) **tia** (aunt-in-law)
    TEE-ah

Você é realmente filha do seu pai!
You really are your father's daughter!

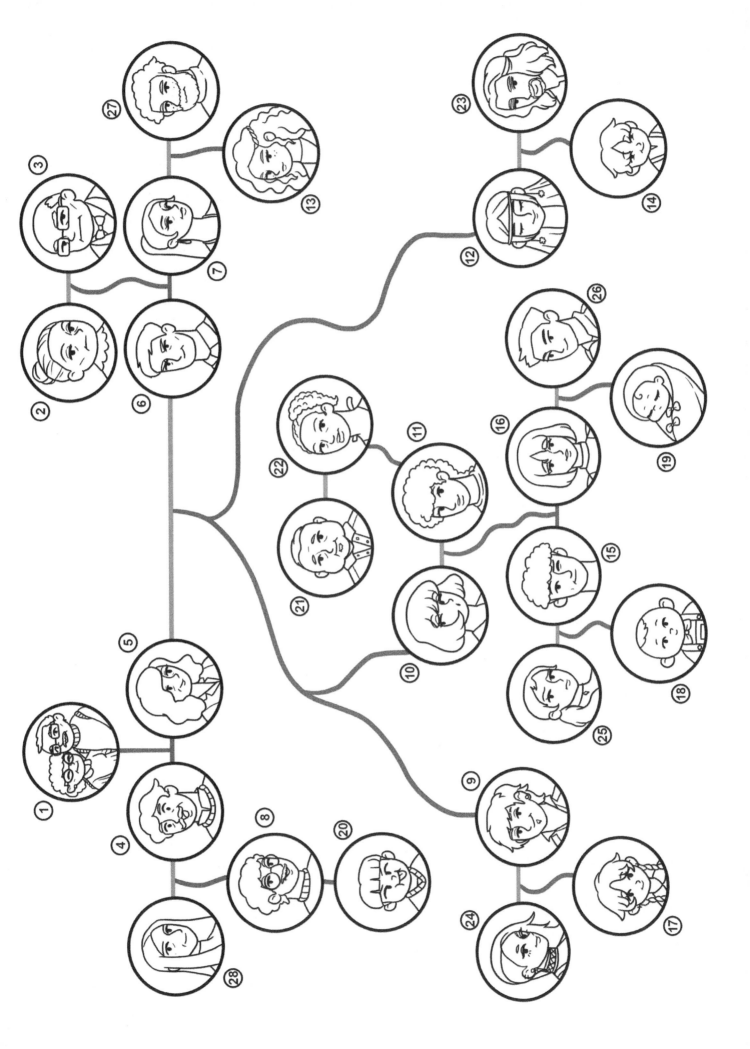

RELACIONAMENTOS (RELATIONSHIPS)

1) **casal casado** (married couple)
   kah-ZAH-oo kah-ZAH-doo

2) **homem casado** (married man)
   OMEM kah-ZAH-doo

3) **mulher casada** (married woman)
   moo-LLIER kah-ZAH-dah

4) **casal divorciado** (divorced couple)
   kah-ZAH-oo dee-voer-see-AH-doo

5) **ex-mulher** (ex-wife)
   ez-moo-LLIER

6) **ex-marido** (ex-husband)
   ez-mah-REE-doo

7) **amigo/amiga** (male/female friend)
   ah-MEE-goo / ah-MEE-gah

8) **namorada** (girlfriend)
   nah-moe-RAH-dah

9) **namorado** (boyfriend)
   nah-moe-RAH-doo

10) **vizinho/vizinha**
    (male/female neighbor)
    vee-ZEE-gnoo / vee-ZEE-gnah

11) **solteiro/solteira** (single man/woman)
    soul-TAY-roo / soul-TAY-rah

12) **divorciada/divorciado**
    (divorcée/divorcé)
    dee-voer-see-AH-dah /
    dee-voer-see-AH-doo

13) **viúvo** (widower)
    vee-OO-voe

14) **viúva** (widow)
    vee-OO-vah

Pauline tem um novo namorado.
Pauline has a new boyfriend.

Eu estou solteiro desde o ano passado.
I have been single since last year.

Meu vizinho é muito barulhento.
My neighbor is very noisy.

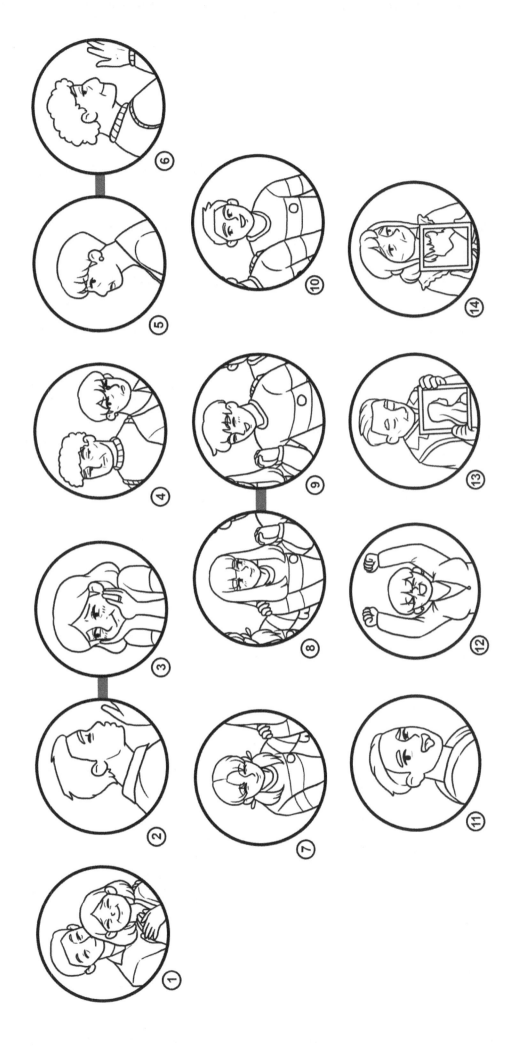

VALORES (VALUES)

1) **respeito** (respect)
   hez-PAY-toe

2) **gratidão** (gratitude)
   grah-chee-DUH-oo

3) **tolerância** (tolerance)
   toe-lea-RUN-see-ah

4) **colaboração** (collaboration)
   koe-lah-boe-rah-SUH-oo

5) **honestidade** (honesty)
   oe-nez-chee-DAH-dee

6) **temperança** (temperance)
   tem-pea-RUN-sah

7) **responsabilidade** (responsibility)
   hez-pon-sah-bee-lee-DAH-dee

8) **fé** (faith)
   FEH

9) **coragem** (courage)
   koe-RAH-zhem

10) **bondade** (kindness)
    bon-DAH-dee

11) **comprometimento** (commitment)
    kom-proe-mea-chee-MAN-too

12) **entusiasmo** (enthusiasm)
    en-tooh-zee-AHZ-moo

13) **confiança** (trust)
    kon-fee-UN-sah

14) **pontualidade** (punctuality)
    pon-tooh-ah-lee-DAH-dee

Honestidade é muito importante em um relacionamento.
Honesty is very important in a relationship.

Eu confio em você.
I trust you.

Eu tenho muitas responsabilidades no trabalho.
I have a lot of responsibilities at work.

O CORPO HUMANO (THE HUMAN BODY)

1) **cabeça** (head)
kah-BEA-sah

2) **cabelo** (hair)
kah-BEA-loo

3) **rosto** (face)
HOZ-toe

4) **testa** (forehead)
TEZ-tah

5) **ouvido** (ear)
oh-VEE-doo

6) **olhos** (eyes)
OEH-llioz

7) **nariz** (nose)
nah-REEZ

8) **bochecha** (cheek)
boe-SHEAH-shah

9) **boca** (mouth)
BOE-kah

10) **queixo** (chin)
KAY-shoo

11) **pescoço** (neck)
pez-KOE-soe

12) **costas** (back)
KOZ-tahz

13) **peito** (chest)
PAY-too

14) **ombro** (shoulder)
OM-broe

15) **braço** (arm)
BRAH-soe

16) **antebraço** (forearm)
un-chee-BRAH-soo

17) **mão** (hand)
MUH-oo

18) **abdômen** (abdomen)
ah-bee-DOE-men

19) **cintura** (waist)
seen-TOO-rah

20) **quadril** (hip)
kwa-DREEW

21) **perna** (leg)
PEAR-nah

22) **coxa** (thigh)
KOE-shah

23) **joelho** (knee)
zhoe-EAH-llio

24) **panturrilha** (calf)
pun-too-HEE-lliah

25) **canela** (shin)
kah-NEA-lah

26) **pé** (foot)
PEH

Eu quebrei meu braço quando tinha 7 anos de idade.
I broke my arm when I was 7 years old.

Suas costas ainda doem?
Does your back still hurt?

Ele chutou minha canela.
He kicked me in the shin.

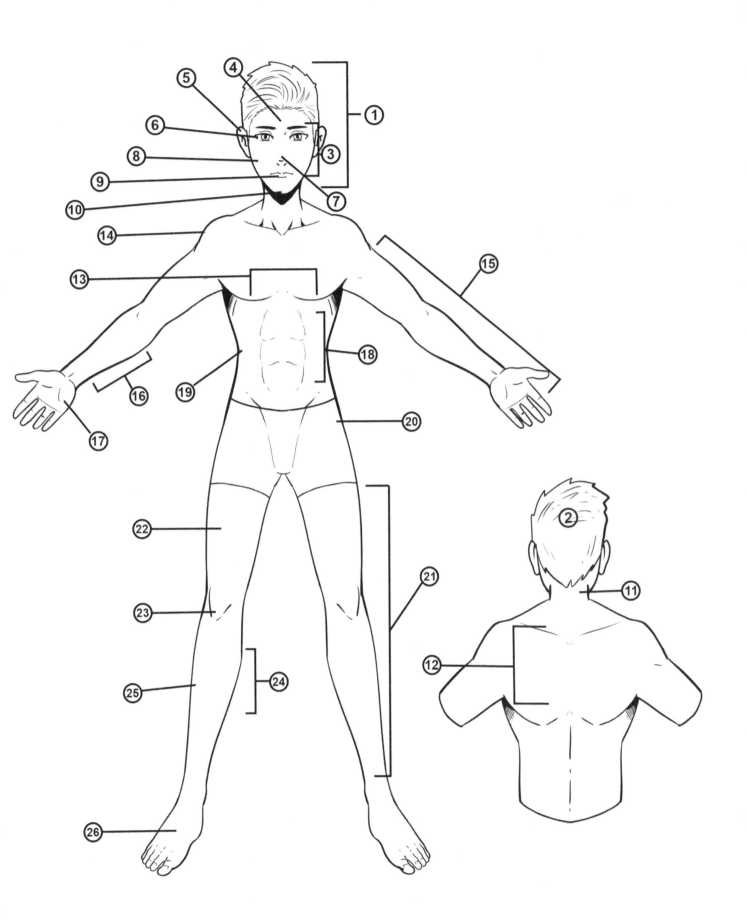

DENTRO DO CORPO HUMANO (INSIDE THE HUMAN BODY)

1) **pele** (skin)
PEH-lee

2) **músculos** (muscles)
MOOZ-koo-looz

3) **ossos** (bones)
AW-soez

4) **cérebro** (brain)
SEH-rea-broe

5) **tireoide** (thyroid)
tee-reah-AW-ee-dee

6) **veias** (veins)
VAY-ahz

7) **artérias** (arteries)
arh-TEH-ree-ahz

8) **coração** (heart)
koe-rah-SUH-oo

9) **pulmões** (lungs)
pool-MOE-eez

10) **estômago** (stomach)
ez-TOE-mah-goe

11) **esôfago** (esophagus)
eah-ZOE-fah-goe

12) **pâncreas** (pancreas)
PUN-creah-ahz

13) **fígado** (liver)
FEE-gah-doo

14) **intestino delgado** (small intestine)
in-tez-CHEE-noo deah-oo-GAH-doo

15) **intestino grosso** (large intestine)
in-tez-CHEE-noo GROE-soe

16) **vesícula biliar** (gallbladder)
veah-ZEE-koo-lah bee-lee-ARH

17) **rins** (kidneys)
HEENZ

18) **bexiga** (urinary bladder)
bea-SHEE-gah

Eu operei meus rins.
I had an operation on my kidneys.

Fumar é ruim para os pulmões.
Smoking is bad for the lungs.

Eu tenho azia.
I have heartburn.

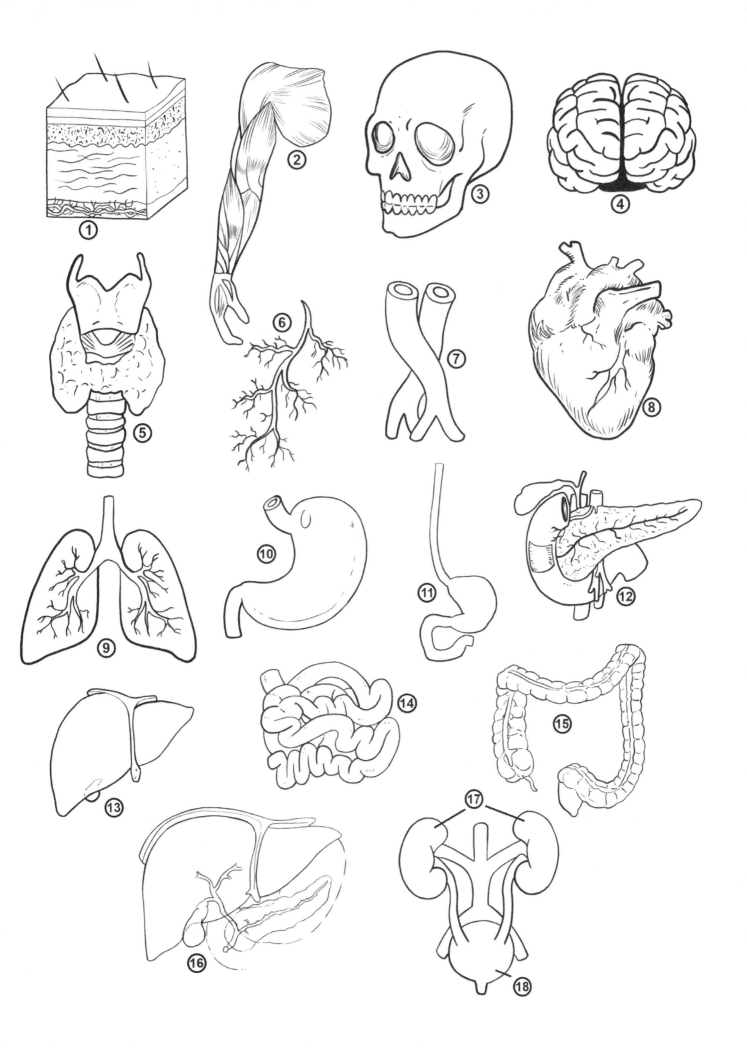

ANIMAIS DE ESTIMAÇÃO (PETS)

1) **cachorro** (dog)
   kah-SHOE-hoe

2) **gato** (cat)
   GAH-toe

3) **furão** (ferret)
   foo-RUH-oo

4) **miniporco** (mini pig/teacup pig)
   mee-nee-POEHR-koe

5) **cavalo** (horse)
   kah-VAH-loo

6) **peixe-anjo** (angelfish)
   pay-shee-UN-zhoo

7) **peixe-palhaço** (clown fish)
   pay-shee-pah-LLIAH-soo

8) **peixinho dourado** (goldfish)
   pay-shee-gnoo dough-RAH-doo

9) **hamster** (hamster)
   HUMZ-teahr

10) **porquinho-da-índia** (guinea pig)
    poehr-KEE-gnoo DA HIN-dee-ah

11) **camundongo** (mouse)
    kah-moon-DON-go

12) **coelho** (rabbit)
    koe-EAH-llio

13) **ouriço** (hedgehog)
    oh-REE-soo

14) **tarântula** (tarantula)
    tah-RUN-too-lah

15) **formigueiro** (ant colony)
    foer-MEE-gueh-roo

16) **cágado** (tortoise)
    KAH-gah-doo

17) **cobra** (snake)
    KOH-brah

18) **camaleão** (chameleon)
    kah-mah-lee-UH-oo

19) **iguana** (iguana)
    ee-GWA-nah

20) **canário** (canary)
    kah-NAH-ree-oe

21) **papagaio** (parrot)
    pah-pah-GAH-ee-oo

22) **periquito** (parakeet)
    peah-ree-KEE-too

Eu prefiro cachorros a gatos.
I prefer dogs over cats.

Eu dei um peixinho dourado para a minha filha.
I gifted a goldfish to my daughter.

Nós devemos salvar os cágados.
We must save the tortoises.

O ZOOLÓGICO (THE ZOO)

1) **elefante** (elephant)
ea-leah-FUN-chee

2) **rinoceronte** (rhino)
hee-noe-seah-RON-chee

3) **girafa** (giraffe)
zhee-RAH-fah

4) **zebra** (zebra)
ZEAH-brah

5) **hipopótamo** (hippopotamus)
ee-poe-POEH-tah-moe

6) **guepardo** (cheetah)
geah-PARH-doe

7) **tigre** (tiger)
CHEE-greah

8) **leão** (lion)
leah-UH-oo

9) **chimpanzé** (chimpanzee)
sheem-pun-ZEAH

10) **orangotango** (orangutan)
oe-run-goe-TUN-goo

11) **babuíno** (baboon)
bah-boo-EE-noe

12) **canguru** (kangaroo)
kun-goo-ROO

13) **coala** (koala)
koe-AH-lah

14) **lêmure** (lemur)
LEAH-moo-ree

O leão é o rei dos animais.
The lion is the king of animals.

Eu fiz carinho em um coala na Austrália.
I petted a koala in Australia.

Os elefantes são muito inteligentes.
Elephants are very intelligent.

PÁSSAROS (BIRDS)

1) **avestruz** (ostrich)
   ah-vez-TROOZ

2) **pavão** (peacock)
   pah-VUH-oo

3) **peru** (turkey)
   peah-ROO

4) **galo** (rooster)
   GAH-loo

5) **pato** (duck)
   PAH-too

6) **cisne** (swan)
   SIS-knee

7) **pelicano** (pelican)
   peah-lee-KUH-noo

8) **flamingo** (flamingo)
   flah-MEEN-goo

9) **pombo** (pigeon)
   POM-boe

10) **coruja** (owl)
    koe-ROO-zhah

11) **abutre** (vulture)
    ah-BOO-tree

12) **águia** (eagle)
    AH-gee-ah

13) **gaivota** (seagull)
    gaee-VOEH-tah

14) **corvo** (crow)
    KORH-voo

15) **tucano** (toucan)
    too-KUH-noo

16) **pinguim** (penguin)
    peen-GWEEN

17) **pica-pau** (woodpecker)
    pee-kah-POW

18) **arara** (macaw)
    ah-RAH-rah

19) **beija-flor** (hummingbird)
    bay-zhah-FLOERH

20) **kiwi** (kiwi)
    kee-WEE

O galo é o símbolo da França.
The rooster is the symbol of France.

Ele é tão orgulhoso quanto um pavão.
He is proud as a peacock.

Nós vamos comer peru no Natal.
We are going to eat turkey for Christmas.

QUIZ #1

Use arrows to match the corresponding translations:

a. goldfish

b. leg

c. brother

d. serious

e. flamingo

f. mouse

g. cheetah

h. neighbor

i. cat

j. sad

k. kindness

l. grandson

m. girlfriend

n. curious

o. brain

p. nose

1. triste

2. neto

3. nariz

4. cérebro

5. bondade

6. guepardo

7. curioso

8. gato

9. flamingo

10. irmão

11. perna

12. camundongo

13. peixinho dourado

14. vizinho

15. sério

16. namorada

Fill in the blank spaces with the options below (use each word only once):

Minha _____ e meu pai estão separados há anos. Todo mundo fica _____ com o quanto eles se dão bem para um _____. Minha _____ é minha melhor amiga. Ela é _____ e tem um _____ de ouro. Eu sou _____, e todo mundo diz que tenho muita _____. Eu gosto de animais, especialmente _____. Fomos convidados para jantar na casa do meu pai amanhã à noite. Eu acho que ele vai preparar um _____. Eu espero estar me sentindo melhor, porque hoje minha _____ dói e meu nariz está _____.

surpreso   bondosa

coragem   irmã

cachorros   peru

casal divorciado   entupido

coração   cabeça

mãe   séria

RÉPTEIS E ANFÍBIOS (REPTILES AND AMPHIBIANS)

- **Répteis (Reptiles)**
  HEAH-pee-tayz

1) **anaconda** (anaconda)
   ah-nah-KOHN-dah

2) **cobra-real** (king cobra)
   KOH-brah heah-OW

3) **cascavel** (rattlesnake)
   kaz-kah-VEH-oo

4) **cobra-coral** (coral snake)
   KOH-brahkoe-RAH-oo

5) **lagarto-de-chifre** (horned lizard)
   lah-GARH-too DEE SHEE-free

6) **lagarto-de-gola** (frill-necked lizard)
   lah-GARH-too DEE GOE-lah

7) **basilisco** (common basilisk/Jesus
   Christ lizard)
   bah-zee-LEEZ-koo

8) **dragão-de-komodo** (Komodo dragon)
   drah-GUH-oo DEE koh-MOEH-doo

9) **crocodilo** (crocodile)
   kroe-koe-DEE-loo

10) **gavial** (gharial/gavial)
    gah-vee-OW

11) **tartaruga marinha** (sea turtle)
    tarh-tah-ROO-gah mah-REE-gnah

- **Anfíbios (Amphibians)**
  Un-FEE-bee-ooz

12) **salamandra** (salamander)
    sah-lah-MUN-drah

13) **rã-golias** (Goliath frog)
    hun-goe-LEE-az

Este rio é cheio de crocodilos.
This river is full of crocodiles.

Eu tenho um dragão-de-komodo em meu viveiro.
I have a Komodo dragon in my vivarium.

Nós devemos proteger as tartarugas da poluição.
We must protect sea turtles from pollution.

INSETOS E ARACNÍDEOS (INSECTS AND ARACHNIDS)

- **Insetos (Insects)**
  in-SEH-toos

1) **abelha** (bee)
   ah-BEAH-llia

2) **mamangava** (bumblebee)
   mah-mun-GAH-vah

3) **vespa** (wasp)
   VEZ-pah

4) **besouro** (beetle)
   bee-ZO-roo

5) **borboleta** (butterfly)
   boer-boe-LEA-tah

6) **mariposa** (moth)
   mah-ree-POE-za

7) **libélula** (dragonfly)
   lee-BEH-loo-lah

8) **joaninha** (ladybug)
   zhoe-uh-KNEE-gnah

9) **vaga-lume** (firefly)
   vah-gah-LOO-mee

10) **barata** (cockroach)
    bah-RAH-tah

11) **mutuca** (horsefly)
    moo-TOOH-kah

12) **mosca** (fly)
    MOEZ-kah

13) **mosquito** (mosquito)
    moz-KEE-too

14) **gafanhoto** (grasshopper)
    gah-FUN-gnoe-toe

15) **grilo** (cricket)
    GREE-loo

- **Aracnídeos (Arachnids)**
  Ah-rah-kee-KNEE-dee-ooz

16) **escorpião** (scorpion)
    ez-koer-pee-UH-oo

17) **aranha** (spider)
    ah-ruh-GNAH

18) **viúva-negra** (Southern black widow)
    vee-OOH-vah-NEAH-grah

Eu odeio aranhas.
I hate spiders.

Eu fui picado por uma vespa.
I got stung by a wasp.

Joaninhas trazem boa sorte.
Ladybugs bring good luck.

MAMÍFEROS I (MAMMALS I)

1) **morcego** (bat)
moerh-SEAH-goo

2) **ornitorrinco** (platypus)
oerh-neen-toe-HEEN-koo

3) **orca** (killer whale/orca)
OHR-kah

4) **golfinho** (dolphin)
go-FEE-gnoo

5) **castor** (beaver)
kaz-TOERH

6) **marmota** (groundhog)
mahr-MOH-tah

7) **toupeira** (mole)
toll-PAY-rah

8) **esquilo** (squirrel)
ez-KEE-loo

9) **doninha** (weasel)
doe-KNEE-gnah

10) **possum** (possum/opossum)
PAW-soom

11) **rato** (rat)
hah-too

12) **lebre** (hare)
LEH-bree

13) **texugo** (badger)
teah-SHOO-goo

14) **gambá** (skunk)
gun-BAH

15) **leopardo** (leopard)
leah-oeh-PARH-doo

Vampiros se transformam em morcegos.
Vampires turn into bats.

Há um esquilo vermelho na árvore.
There is a red squirrel in the tree.

Olha, ela está com um rato no ombro!
Look, she has a rat on her shoulder!

MAMÍFEROS II (MAMMALS II)

1) **urso** (bear)
OORH-soo

2) **hiena** (hyena)
ee-EAH-nah

3) **chacal** (jackal)
chah-KOW

4) **vaca** (cow)
VAH-kah

5) **touro** (bull)
TOLL-roo

6) **raposa** (fox)
hah-POE-zah

7) **búfalo** (buffalo)
BOOH-fah-loo

8) **alce** (elk/moose)
OW-see

9) **ovelha** (sheep)
oe-VEAH-lliah

10) **cabrito** (goat)
kah-BREE-toe

11) **gazela** (gazelle)
gah-ZEAH-lah

12) **lobo** (wolf)
LOE-boo

13) **macaco** (monkey)
mah-KAH-koo

14) **carneiro** (ram)
karh-NAY-roo

15) **burro** (donkey)
BOO-hooh

Nunca corra na frente de um urso.
Never run in front of a bear.

A Chapeuzinho Vermelho foi comida por um lobo.
Little Red Riding Hood was eaten by a wolf.

Minha vaca me dá leite todos os dias.
My cow gives me milk every day.

41

PEIXES E MOLUSCOS (FISH AND MOLLUSKS)

- **Peixes (Fish)**
  PAY-shees

1) **tubarão-baleia** (whale shark)
   too-bah-RUH-oo bah-LAY-ah

2) **tubarão branco** (white shark)
   too-bah-RUH-oo BRUN-koe

3) **tubarão-martelo** (hammerhead shark)
   too-bah-RUH-oo marh-TEAH-loo

4) **peixe-espada** (swordfish/marlin)
   pay-shee-ez-PAH-dah

5) **barracuda** (barracuda)
   bah-hah-KOO-dah

6) **baiacu** (pufferfish)
   bah-ee-ah-KOO

7) **bagre** (catfish)
   BAH-gree

8) **piranha** (piranha)
   pee-RUH-gna

9) **peixe voador** (flying fish)
   PAY-shee voe-ah-DORH

10) **moreia** (moray eel)
    moe-REH-ee-ah

11) **raia manta** (manta ray)
    HAH-ee-ah MUN-tah

12) **cavalo marinho** (seahorse)
    kah-VAH-loo mah-REE-gnoe

- **Moluscos (Mollusks)**
  Moe-LOOZ-kooz

13) **lula** (squid)
    LOO-lah

14) **choco** (cuttlefish)
    SHOEH-koo

15) **polvo** (octopus)
    POE-voo

16) **ostra** (oyster)
    OZ-trah

17) **mariscos** (clam)
    mah-REEZ-koz

18) **nautilus** (nautilus)
    NOW-tee-looz

19) **caramujo** (snail)
    kah-rah-MOO-zhoo

20) **lesma** (slug)
    LEZ-mah

Cuidado com os tubarões brancos.
Beware of the white sharks.

Eu odeio comer ostras.
I hate eating oysters.

Meu irmão pegou um bagre enorme.
My brother caught a huge catfish.

ROUPAS I (CLOTHING I)

1) **capa de chuva** (raincoat)
   KAH-pah DEE SHOO-vah

2) **moletom com capuz** (hoodie)
   moe-leah-TOM KOM kah-POOZ

3) **jaqueta** (jacket)
   zhah-KEAH-tah

4) **jeans** (jeans)
   JEANS

5) **samba-canção** (boxer shorts)
   sun-bah-kun-SUH-oo

6) **botas** (boots)
   BOH-tahz

7) **brincos** (earrings)
   BREEN-kooz

8) **suéter** (sweater)
   soo-EH-teahr

9) **colar** (necklace)
   coe-LAHR

10) **sutiã** (bra)
    soo-chee-UN

11) **leggings** (leggings)
    LEH-geenz

12) **meias** (socks)
    MAY-ahz

13) **blusa** (blouse/top)
    BLOO-zah

14) **pulseira** (bracelet)
    pool-SAY-rah

15) **short** (shorts)
    SHOHRT

16) **calcinha** (panties)
    cow-see-GNAH

17) **casaco** (coat)
    kah-ZAH-koo

18) **vestido** (dress)
    vez-TEE-doo

19) **bolsa** (purse)
    BOW-sah

20) **sandálias** (sandals)
    sun-DAH-lliaz

Não esqueça sua capa de chuva!
Do not forget your raincoat!

Tem um buraco na minha meia.
There is a hole in my sock.

Se estiver com frio, vista um suéter.
If you are cold, wear a sweater.

ROUPAS II (CLOTHING II)

1) **chapéu** (hat)
shah-PEH-oo

2) **smoking** (tuxedo/smoking)
SMO-king

3) **gravata borboleta** (bow tie)
grah-VAH-tah boerh-boe-LEAH-tah

4) **sapatos** (shoes)
sah-PAH-toos

5) **terno** (suit)
TEHR-noo

6) **camisa** (shirt)
kah-MEE-zah

7) **gravata** (tie)
grah-VAH-tah

8) **pasta** (briefcase/case)
PAHZ-tah

9) **blusa de manga comprida** (long-sleeved blouse)
BLOO-zah DEE MUN-gah KOM-pree-dah

10) **top** (sports bra)
TOHP

11) **calças** (trousers/pants)
KOW-sahs

12) **cinto** (belt)
SEEN-too

13) **anel** (ring)
ah-NEAH-oo

14) **camiseta** (T-shirt)
kah-MEE-zeh-tah

15) **saia** (skirt)
SAH-yah

16) **cachecol** (scarf)
kah-shee-KOLL

17) **relógio** (watch)
heah-LAW-zhee-oe

18) **calça cargo** (cargo pants)
KOW-sah KAHR-goo

19) **carteira** (wallet)
karh-TAY-tah

20) **guarda-chuva** (umbrella)
gwarh-dah-SHOO-vah

O dinheiro está na pasta.
The money is in the briefcase.

O sol está forte, você deve usar um chapéu.
The sun is shining, you must wear a hat.

Eu perdi meu relógio.
I have lost my watch.

O CLIMA (THE WEATHER)

1) **ensolarado** (sunny)
   an-soe-lah-RAH-doo

2) **quente** (hot)
   KAN-chee

3) **tempestade de areia** (sandstorm)
   tem-peahz-TAH-dee DEE ah-RAY-ah

4) **nublado** (cloudy)
   noo-BLAH-doo

5) **calor** (warm)
   kah-LORH

6) **nebuloso** (foggy/misty)
   nea-boo-LOE-zoo

7) **chovendo** (rainy)
   shoo-VEN-doo

8) **fresco** (cool)
   FRAYZ-koo

9) **gota de chuva** (raindrop)
   goe-tah-dee-SHOO-vah

10) **úmido** (humid)
    OOH-mee-doo

11) **tempestade** (storm)
    tem-peahz-TAH-dee

12) **raio** (lightning)
    HAH-yo

13) **ventando** (windy)
    ven-TUN-doo

14) **nevando** (snowy)
    nea-VUN-doo

15) **frio** (cold)
    FREE-oo

16) **floco de neve** (snowflake)
    flaw-koe dee NEAH-vee

É muito quente em Dubai.
It is very hot in Dubai.

Eu estou com frio.
I am cold.

Nós não podemos entrar no deserto devido à tempestade de areia.
We cannot go into the desert because of a sandstorm.

AS ESTAÇÕES – PRIMAVERA (THE SEASONS – SPRING)

1) **jardim** (garden)
   zharh-DEEM

2) **desabrochar** (blossom)
   dea-zah-broe-SHARH

3) **piquenique** (picnic)
   peek-NEEK

4) **parque** (park)
   PAHR-kee

5) **passeio de bicicleta** (bike ride)
   pah-SAY-oh DEE bee-see-KLEH-tah

6) **limonada** (lemonade)
   lee-moe-NAH-dah

7) **venda de garagem** (garage sale)
   VEN-dah DEE gah-rah-ZHEM

8) **road trip** (road trip)
   ROAD TRIP

9) **pintar pedras** (to paint rocks)
   peen-TAHR PEAH-drahz

10) **plantar flores** (to plant some flowers)
    plun-TAHR FLOE-reez

11) **soltar pipa** (to fly a kite)
    soul-TAHR PEE-pah

12) **ir a um churrasco** (to attend a barbecue)
    EERH AH OOM SHOO-hahz-koo

Sábado faremos um piquenique no parque.
Saturday, we are going to have a picnic in the park.

Eu sonho em fazer uma road trip pela América.
I dream of going on a road trip through America.

Nós amamos fazer passeios de bicicleta nos Alpes.
We love bike rides in the Alps.

AS ESTAÇÕES – VERÃO (THE SEASONS – SUMMER)

1) **acampar** (to go camping)
   ah-kum-PAHR

2) **parque aquático** (water park)
   PAHR-kee ah-KWAH-chee-koe

3) **atividades ao ar livre** (outdoor activities)
   ah-chee-vee-DAH-deez OW AHR LEE-vree

4) **piscina** (swimming pool)
   pee-SEE-nah

5) **nadar** (to swim)
   nah-DARH

6) **se bronzear** (to get tanned)
   SEE brom-zee-ARH

7) **protetor solar** (sunscreen)
   proe-teah-TOHR soe-lahr

8) **repelente** (insect repellent)
   heah-peah-LEN-chee

9) **lago** (lake)
   LAH-goo

10) **salva-vidas** (lifesaver/lifeguard)
    sah-oo-vah-VEE-dahz

11) **castelo de areia** (sandcastle)
    kaz-TEAH-loo DEE ah-RAY-a

12) **fazer uma trilha** (to go on a hike)
    fah-ZEARH OO-mah TREE-lliah

O Lago Annecy é muito bonito.
The Annecy Lake is beautiful.

Eu amo me bronzear na praia.
I love to tan on the beach.

Não esqueça seu protetor solar!
Do not forget your sunscreen!

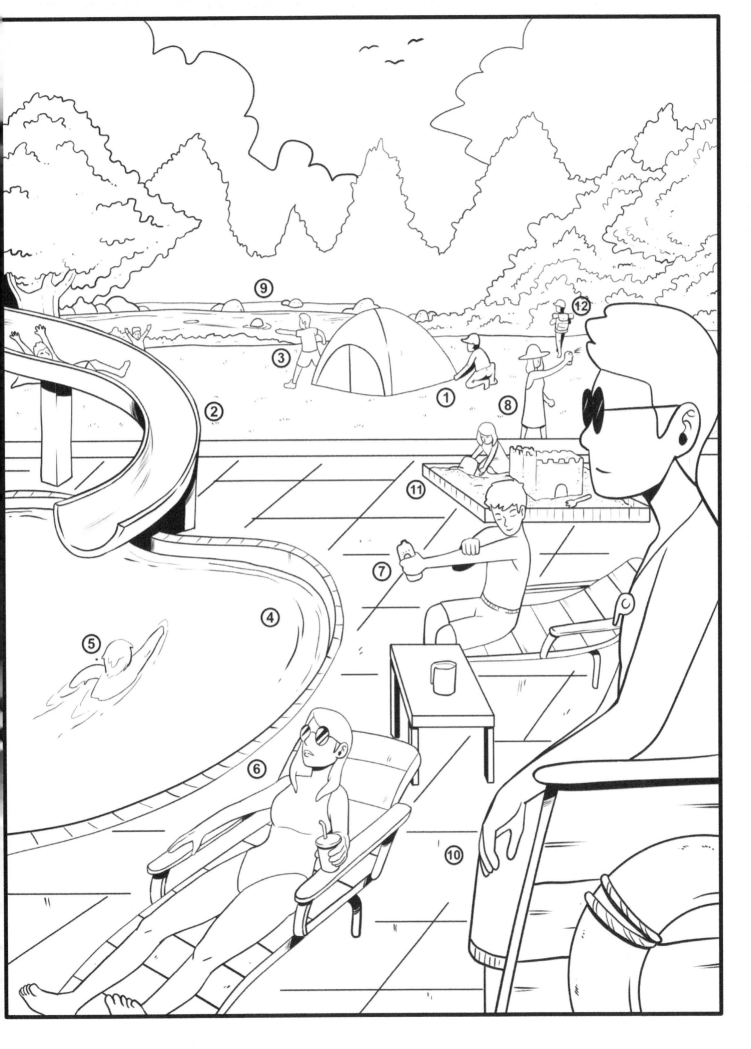

QUIZ #2

Use arrows to match the corresponding translations:

a. horsefly

b. squirrel

c. king cobra

d. coat

e. socks

f. Komodo dragon

g. tie

h. slug

i. trousers/pants

j. snail

k. sunny

l. beetle

m. bat

n. cold

o. necklace

p. butterfly

1. ensolarado

2. meias

3. calças

4. besouro

5. esquilo

6. morcego

7. frio

8. cobra-real

9. casaco

10. mutuca

11. colar

12. caramujo

13. dragão-de-komodo

14. borboleta

15. gravata

16. lesma

Fill in the blank spaces with the options below (use each word only once):

Lisa é professora de jardim de infância. Na semana passada, ela levou a turma a uma fazenda. A previsão dizia que ia chover, mas estava muito _____. O dia inteiro foi _____ . Lisa vestiu _____, _____ e um grande _____. Infelizmente, ela se sentiu desconfortável o dia inteiro. Durante a visita à fazenda, as crianças viram porcos, cavalos e _____. Havia também uma colmeia com centenas de _____. Também havia _____, e uma delas picou a Lisa!

calças   abelhas

sapatos   ensolarado

vespas   vacas

calor   casaco

AS ESTAÇÕES – OUTONO (THE SEASONS – FALL/AUTUMN)

1) **folhas caindo** (falling leaves)
   FOE-lliaz kah-IN-doo

2) **juntar folhas** (to collect leaves)
   zhoon-TAHR FOE-lliaz

3) **abóbora** (pumpkin)
   ah-BOH-boe-rah

4) **decorar uma abóbora** (to carve a
   pumpkin)
   deah-koeh-RAHR OOH-mah ah-BOH-
   boe-rah

5) **colher maçãs** (apple picking)
   koe-LLIEAHR mah-SUNS

6) **fantasia de Halloween** (Halloween
   costume)
   fun-tah-ZEE-ah DEE hah-low-IN

7) **doces de Halloween** (Halloween
   candy)
   DOEH-sees DEE hah-low-IN

8) **velas aromatizadas** (spiced candles)
   VEAH-lahz ah-roe-mah-chee-ZAH-
   daz

9) **jantar de Ação de Graças**
   (Thanksgiving dinner)
   zhun-TAHR DEE ah-SUH-oo DEE
   GRAH-saz

10) **manta de lã** (wool blanket)
    MUN-tuh DEE LUN

11) **assar marshmallows** (to roast
    marshmallows)
    ah-sahr MARSH-meh-lows

12) **decorar o quintal** (to decorate the
    yard)
    deah-koe-RAHR OO keen-TOW

Eu decorei uma abóbora para o Halloween.
I carved a pumpkin for Halloween.

Eu comprei velas aromatizadas para o Natal.
I bought spiced candles for Christmas.

Em dezembro, eu começo a decorar o quintal.
In December, I start to decorate the yard.

AS ESTAÇÕES – INVERNO (THE SEASONS – WINTER)

1) **chocolate quente** (hot cocoa/hot chocolate)
sho-koe-LAH-chee kem-CHEE

2) **trenó** (sled)
treah-NOH

3) **luvas** (mittens)
LOO-vahz

4) **jaqueta puffer** (puffer jacket)
zhah-KEAH-tah puh-feahr

5) **sopa** (soup)
SOE-pah

6) **biscoitos de gengibre** (gingerbread cookies)
beez-KO-ee-toes DEE zhen-ZEE-bree

7) **janela embaçada** (frosty window)
zhah-NEAH-lah am-bah-SAH-dah

8) **pinha** (pinecone)
PEE-gnah

9) **esquiar no gelo** (ice skating)
ez-kee-AHR NOO ZHE-loo

10) **esquiar** (ski)
ez-kee-AHR

11) **pista de gelo** (ice rink)
PEEZ-tah DEE ZHE-loo

12) **bola de neve** (snowball)
BAW-lah DEE NEH-vee

Eu amo beber chocolate quente perto da lareira.
I love to drink hot chocolate near the fire.

Eu comecei a esquiar com quatro anos.
I started skiing at the age of 4.

A sopa está pronta.
The soup is ready.

AS HORAS (TIME)

1) **fuso horário** (time zone)
   FOO-zoo oe-RAH-ree-oo

2) **segundo** (second)
   seah-GOON-doo

3) **minuto** (minute)
   mee-NOO-toe

4) **hora** (hour)
   OH-rah

5) **dia** (day)
   DEE-ah

6) **semana** (week)
   seah-MAH-nah

7) **quinzena** (fortnight)
   keem-ZEAH-nah

8) **mês** (month)
   MAYZ

9) **ano** (year)
   uh-NOEH

10) **amanhecer** (dawn)
    ah-muh-gneah-SEAHR

11) **manhã** (morning)
    muh-GNAH

12) **meio-dia** (noon/midday)
    MAY-oo DEE-ah

13) **tarde** (afternoon)
    TARH-dee

14) **escurecer** (dusk)
    ez-koo-reah-SEARH

15) **noite** (night)
    NO-ee-chee

16) **meia-noite** (midnight)
    may-ah-NOE-ee-chee

17) **data** (date)
    DAH-tah

18) **calendário** (calendar)
    kah-len-DAH-ree-oo

Minha filha acorda frequentemente à noite.
My daughter wakes up often at night.

Quando é o seu aniversário?
When is your birthday?

Nós te esperamos ao meio-dia para o almoço.
We expect you at 12 p.m. for lunch.

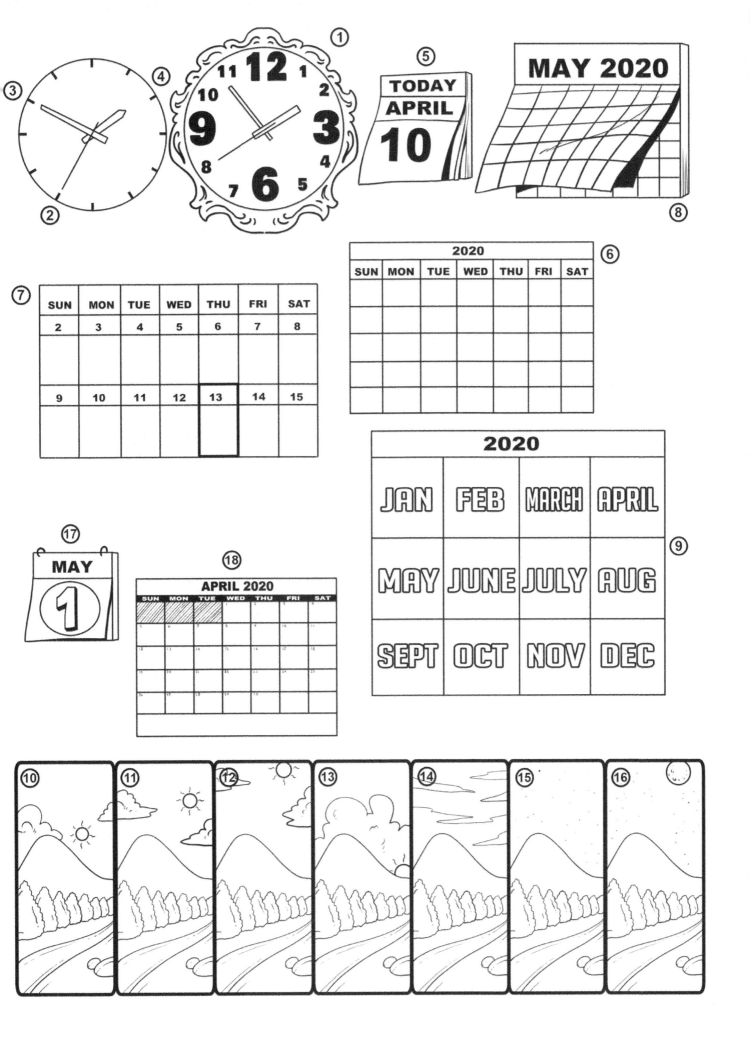

A CASA (THE HOUSE)

1) **sótão** (attic)
SAW-tuh-oo

2) **telhado** (roof)
teah-LLIAH-doo

3) **teto** (ceiling)
TEAH-too

4) **chaminé** (chimney)
shah-mee-NEH

5) **parede** (wall)
pah-REAH-dee

6) **sacada** (balcony)
sah-KAH-dah

7) **varanda** (porch)
vah-RUN-dah

8) **janela** (window)
zha-NEH-lah

9) **persianas** (shutters)
peahr-see-UH-nahs

10) **porta** (door)
POORH-tah

11) **escada** (stairs)
ez-KAH-dah

12) **corrimão** (banister)
koe-hee-MUH-oo

13) **chão** (floor)
SHUH-oo

14) **porão** (basement)
poe-RUH-oo

15) **quintal** (backyard)
keen-TOW

16) **garagem** (garage)
gah-RAH-zhem

17) **entrada de carro** (driveway)
en-TRAH-dah DEE KAH-hoo

18) **cerca** (fence/picket fence)
sehr-kah

19) **caixa de correio** (mailbox)
KAH-ee-sha DEE koe-HAY-oo

20) **corredor** (hallway/corridor)
koe-heah-DORH

Tem teias de aranha no teto.
There are cobwebs on the ceiling.

Seu quintal é muito bonito.
Your backyard is very beautiful.

Eu caí da escada.
I fell down the stairs.

ITENS DE COZINHA (KITCHEN ITEMS)

1) **fogão** (stove)
foeh-GUH-oo

2) **micro-ondas** (microwave oven)
mee-kroe-ON-dahz

3) **forno elétrico** (toaster oven)
FOERH-noe ea-LEH-tree-koo

4) **mixer** (electric mixer)
MEE-ksear

5) **liquidificador** (blender)
lee-quee-dee-fee-kah-DOERH

6) **torradeira** (toaster)
toe-hah-DAY-rah

7) **cafeteira** (coffee maker)
kah-feah-TAY-rah

8) **geladeira** (fridge)
zheah-lah-DAY-rah

9) **despensa** (pantry)
deez-PEN-sah

10) **armário** (cupboard)
ahr-MAHR-ree-oe

11) **forma de bolo** (cake pan)
FOERH-mah DEE BOE-loo

12) **frigideira** (frying pan)
free-zhee-DAY-rah

13) **panela** (pot)
pah-NEH-lah

14) **formas de biscoito** (cookie cutters)
FOERH-mahs DEE beez-KOY-too

15) **tigela** (mixing bowl)
tee-ZHEH-lah

16) **escorredor** (colander)
ez-koe-heah-DOEHR

17) **peneira** (strainer)
pea-NAY-rah

18) **rolo de massa** (rolling pin)
HOE-loe DEE MAh-sah

19) **luva de forno** (oven mitt)
LOO-vah DEE FOERH-noe

20) **avental** (apron)
ah-ven-TOW

Eu usei um liquidificador para fazer um smoothie.
I used a blender to make a smoothie.

Pegue um iogurte na geladeira.
Go get a yogurt from the fridge.

Eu abri a massa com um rolo de massa.
I rolled the pastry with a rolling pin.

ITENS DO QUARTO (BEDROOM ITEMS)

1) **cama** (bed)
   KAH-mah

2) **colchão** (mattress)
   kaul-SHU-oo

3) **roupa de cama** (bedding/bed linen)
   HO-pah DEE KAH-mah

4) **travesseiro** (pillow)
   trah-vee-SAY-roo

5) **lençóis** (sheets)
   len-SAW-eez

6) **cobertor** (blanket)
   koe-beahr-TOERH

7) **cobre-leito** (spread)
   koe-bree-LAY-too

8) **fronha** (pillowcase)
   FROE-gnah

9) **criado-mudo** (nightstand)
   kree-AH-doo MOO-doo

10) **relógio de mesa** (table clock)
    heah-LAW-zhee-oe DEE MEAH-zah

11) **luminária** (table light)
    loo-mee-NAH-ree-ah

12) **roupeiro** (closet)
    ho-PAY-roo

13) **cadeira de balanço** (rocking chair)
    kah-DAY-rah DEE bah-LUN-soo

14) **abajur** (lamp)
    ah-bah-ZHOOR

15) **espelho** (mirror)
    ez-PEAH-llio

16) **cômoda** (dresser)
    KOE-moe-dah

17) **cortina** (curtain)
    kor-TEE-nah

18) **berço** (cradle/crib)
    BEAHR-soe

19) **móbile** (crib mobile)
    MOH-bee-lee

20) **cabide** (hanger)
    kah-BEE-dee

Eu vou trocar os lençóis da cama.
I am going to change the bedsheets.

O bebê está em seu berço.
The baby is in his crib.

Este colchão é muito duro para mim.
This mattress is too hard for me.

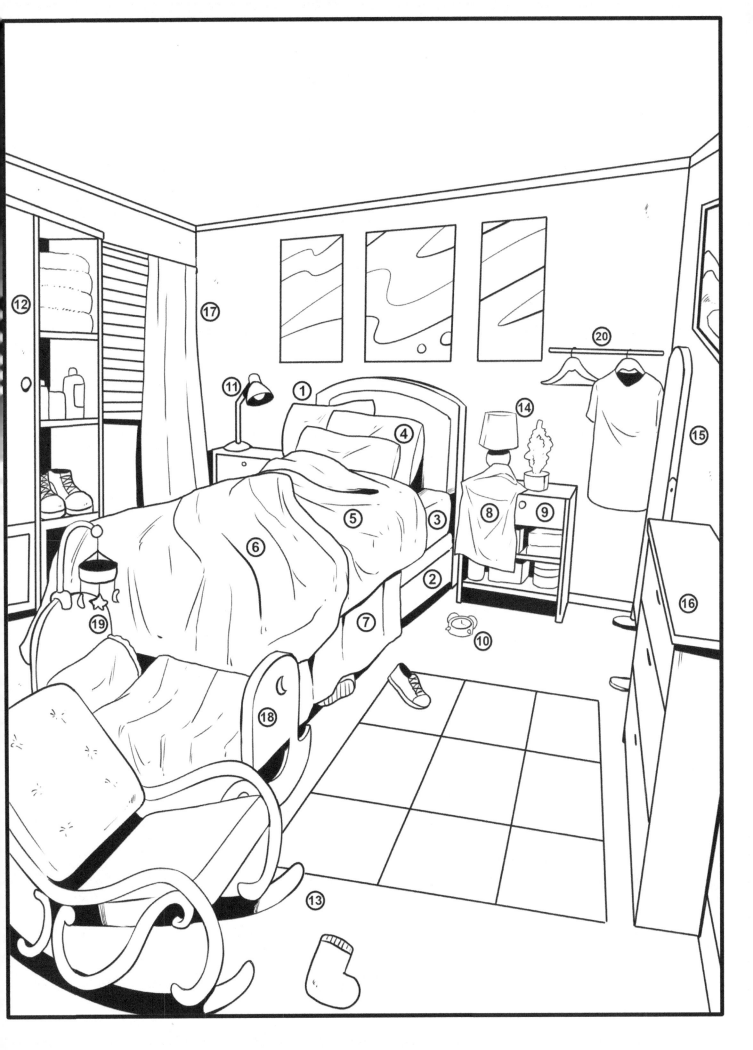

ITENS DO BANHEIRO (BATHROOM ITEMS)

1) **cortina do chuveiro** (shower curtain)
   kor-CHEE-nah DOE xoo-VAY-roo

2) **toalha** (towel)
   toe-AH-llia

3) **suporte de toalha** (towel rack)
   soo-POR-chee DEE toe-AH-llia

4) **toalha de rosto** (hand towel)
   toe-AH-llia DEE HOZ-toeh

5) **banheira** (bathtub)
   bun-GNAY-rah

6) **chuveiro** (shower)
   xoo-VAY-roo

7) **vaso** (toilet/WC)
   VAH-zoo

8) **pia** (sink/washbasin)
   PEE-ah

9) **torneira** (faucet/tap)
   toer-NAY-rah

10) **tapete de banheiro** (bathmat)
   tah-PEAH-chee DEE bun-GNAY-roo

11) **armário de banheiro** (medicine cabinet)
   ar-MAH-ree-oo DEE bun-GNAY-roo

12) **pasta de dente** (toothpaste)
   PAZ-tah DEE DEN-chee

13) **escova de dente** (toothbrush)
   ez-KOEH-vah DEE DEN-chee

14) **xampu** (shampoo)
   SHUM-poo

15) **pente** (comb)
   PEN-chee

16) **sabonete** (soap)
   sah-boe-NEAH-chee

17) **espuma de barbear** (shaving foam)
   ez-POO-mah DEE bar-BEAH-AR

18) **barbeador** (razor/shaver)
   bahr-beh-ah-DOR

19) **papel higiênico** (toilet paper)
   pah-PEAH-oo ee-zhee-EAH-nee-koe

20) **desentupidor** (plunger)
   deah-zen-too-pee-DOR

21) **escova sanitária** (toilet brush)
   ez-KOEH-vah sah-knee-TAH-ree-ah

22) **lixeira** (wastebasket)
   lee-SHAY-rah

Não tem mais papel higiênico!
There is no more toilet paper!

Coloque a tolha de rosto no suporte de toalha.
Place the hand towel on the towel rack.

Não esqueça de fechar a torneira.
Do not forget to turn off the tap.

ITENS DA SALA DE ESTAR (LIVING ROOM ITEMS)

1) **móveis** (furniture)
MOH-vayz

2) **cadeira** (chair)
kah-DAY-rah

3) **sofá** (sofa)
soe-FAH

4) **pufe** (ottoman)
POO-fee

5) **almofada** (cushion)
ahl-moe-FAH-dah

6) **mesa de centro** (coffee table)
MEAH-zah DEE cen-troo

7) **cinzeiro** (ashtray)
seen-ZAY-roo

8) **vaso** (vase)
VAH-zoo

9) **decoração** (ornaments)
deah-koeh-rah-SUH-oo

10) **estante** (bookshelf/bookcase)
ez-TUN-chee

11) **revisteiro** (magazine holder)
heah-veez-TAY-roo

12) **sistema de som** (stereo)
sis-TE-mah DEE SOHM

13) **caixa de som** (speakers)
KAH-ee-shah DEE SOHM

14) **lareira** (fireplace)
lah-RAY-rah

15) **lustre** (chandelier)
LOOZ-tree

16) **abajur** (lamp)
ah-bah-ZHOOR

17) **lâmpada** (light bulb)
LUM-pah-dah

18) **relógio de parede** (wall clock)
heah-LAW-zheeo DEE pah-REAH-dee

19) **quadro** (painting)
KUA-droo

20) **TV/televisão** (TV/television)
teah-VEAH/teah-leah-vee-ZUH-oo

21) **controle remoto** (remote control)
kon-TROE-lee heah-MOH-too

22) **console de videogame** (video game console)
con-so-LEE DEE VEE-dew-GAY-mee

Eu passo muito tempo na frente da TV.
I spend too much time in front of the TV.

Eu comprei um console de videogame para o meu marido no Natal.
I bought my husband a video game console for Christmas.

Estou quase terminando meu primeiro quadro.
I have nearly finished my first painting.

ITENS DA SALA DE JANTAR (DINING ROOM ITEMS)

1) **mesa de jantar** (dining table)
MEAH-zah DEE zhun-TAHR

2) **toalha de mesa** (tablecloth)
toe-AH-llia DEE MEAH-zah

3) **centro de mesa** (centerpiece)
CEN-troo DEE MEAH-zah

4) **jogo americano** (placemat)
ZHOE-goe ah-meah-ree-KUH-noo

5) **prato** (plate)
PRAH-too

6) **guardanapo** (napkin)
gwar-dah-NAH-poo

7) **faca** (knife)
FAH-kah

8) **garfo** (fork)
GAHR-foo

9) **colher** (spoon)
koe-LLIEHR

10) **jarra** (pitcher/jar)
ZHAH-hah

11) **copo** (glass)
KOH-poo

12) **xícara** (mug/cup)
SHEE-kah-rah

13) **saleiro** (saltshaker)
sah-LAY-roo

14) **pimenteiro** (pepper shaker)
pee-men-TAY-roo

15) **bandeja** (tray)
bun-DEAH-zhah

16) **bebida** (drink/beverage)
beah-BEE-dah

17) **comida** (food)
koe-MEE-dah

18) **lanche** (snack)
LUN-shee

Eu vou te trazer o café da manhã em uma bandeja.
I will bring you breakfast on a tray.

Qual centro de mesa você escolheu para o seu casamento?
Which centerpiece have you chosen for your wedding?

Você quer uma bebida?
Do you want a drink?

QUIZ #3

Use arrows to match the corresponding translations:

a. morning

b. pumpkin

c. door

d. Halloween costume

e. pillow

f. afternoon

g. sled

h. apron

i. ice rink

j. towel rack

k. wall

l. closet

m. window

n. fireplace

o. snowball

p. toaster oven

1. janela

2. roupeiro

3. trenó

4. parede

5. avental

6. bola de neve

7. travesseiro

8. fantasia de Halloween

9. porta

10. forno elétrico

11. tarde

12. suporte de toalha

13. pista de gelo

14. abóbora

15. lareira

16. manhã

Fill in the blank spaces with the options below (use each word only once):

O outono é a minha estação favorita. Todos os anos, aguardo com impaciência o mês de outubro, porque decoro o _____. Eu também decoro minha _____. Meus amigos e eu gostamos de esculpir _____ e colocá-las por toda a casa. Eu sempre coloco uma na frente da _____; elas parecem _____ assustadoras! O 31 de outubro é o Halloween. Nesta data, vamos até a casa dos vizinhos para pegar doces. Então, por volta da _____, acendemos _____ e relaxamos no _____ com _____. Às vezes, também jogamos no _____. Em novembro, eu vou _____ na _____ da cidade. Estou animado!

sacada

chocolate quente

meia-noite

lâmpadas

velas perfumadas

console de videogame

abóboras

banco

jardim

esquiar

pista de gelo

lareira

O JARDIM/QUINTAL (THE GARDEN/THE BACKYARD)

1) **jardineiro** (gardener)
zhar-dee-NAY-roo

2) **galpão** (shed)
gal-PUH-oo

3) **arbusto** (bush)
ar-BOOZ-too

4) **gramado** (lawn)
gruh-MAH-doo

5) **grama** (grass)
GRUH-mah

6) **flor** (flower)
FLOER

7) **mangueira** (garden hose)
mun-GAY-rah

8) **regador** (watering can)
heah-gah-DOR

9) **vaso de planta** (flowerpot)
VAH-zoo DEE PLUN-tah

10) **luva de jardinagem** (gardening gloves)
LOO-vah DEE zhar-dee-NAH-zhem

11) **pá** (shovel)
PAH

12) **ancinho** (rake)
un-SEEN-gnoo

13) **garfo de jardinagem** (gardening fork)
GAHR-foo DEE zhar-dee-NAH-zhem

14) **tesoura de poda** (pruners/pruning shears)
teh-ZO-rah DEE POH-dah

15) **espátula de jardinagem** (garden trowel)
ez-PAH-too-lah DEE zhar-dee-NAH-zhem

16) **torneira** (tap)
toer-NAY-rah

17) **carrinho de mão** (wheelbarrow)
kah-HEE-gno DEE MUH-oo

18) **cortador de grama** (lawn mower)
koer-tah-DOR DEE GRUH-mah

19) **lanterna** (lantern)
lun-TEHR-nah

20) **videira** (vine)
vee-DAY-rah

Uma videira cresce em meu jardim.
A vine grows in my garden.

Eu coloquei todas as minhas ferramentas no galpão.
I have put all my tools in the shed.

O carrinho de mão está cheio de folhas mortas.
The wheelbarrow is full of dead leaves.

A ÁREA DE SERVIÇO (THE CLEANING ROOM)

1) **máquina de lavar** (washing machine)
   MAH-kee-nah DEE lah-VAHR

2) **secadora** (dryer)
   seah-kah-DOE-rah

3) **ferro** (iron)
   FEH-hoe

4) **tábua de passar** (ironing board)
   TAH-boo-ah DEE PAH-sahr

5) **sabão** (laundry soap)
   sah-BUH-oo

6) **sabão líquido** (laundry detergent)
   sah-BUH-oo LEE-kee-doo

7) **amaciante de roupas** (fabric softener)
   ah-mah-see-UN-chee DEE HO-pahz

8) **cesto de roupas** (laundry basket)
   SEZ-too DEE HO-pahz

9) **roupa suja** (dirty clothes)
   HO-pah SOO-zhah

10) **roupa limpa** (clean laundry)
    HO-pah LEEM-pah

11) **vassoura** (broom)
    vah-SO-rah

12) **escova e pá de lixo** (brush and dust pan)
    ez-KOE-vah EAH PAH DEE LEE-shoo

13) **luva de borracha** (rubber gloves)
    LOO-vah DEE boe-HAH-shah

14) **esponja** (sponge)
    ez-PON-zhah

15) **bacia de plástico** (plastic tub)
    bah-SEE-ah DEE PLAZH-chee-koo

16) **esfregão** (mop)
    ez-freah-GUH-oo

17) **balde** (bucket)
    BAO-dee

18) **pano de limpeza** (cleaning cloths)
    PUH-noo DEE leem-PEAH-zah

19) **escova de lavar** (scrub brush)
    ez-KOE-vah DEE lah-VAHR

20) **água sanitária** (bleach)
    AH-gwa suh-nee-TAH-ree-ah

21) **desinfetante** (disinfectant)
    deah-zeen-feah-TUN-chee

22) **lata de lixo** (garbage can)
    LAH-ta DEE LEE-shoo

Eu odeio lavar roupa.
I hate doing the laundry.

Você deve passar o esfregão no chão.
You must mop the floor.

Você pode usar amaciante de roupas na máquina de lavar.
You can use fabric softener in the washing machine.

A ESCOLA/A UNIVERSIDADE (THE SCHOOL/THE UNIVERSITY)

1) **professor** (teacher)
proe-feah-SOEHR

2) **aluno** (student)
ah-LOO-noo

3) **sala de aula** (classroom)
SAH-lah DEE OW-lah

4) **armário** (locker)
ahr-MAH-ree-oo

5) **quadro de avisos** (bulletin board)
KWA-droo DEE ah-VEE-zooz

6) **folha de papel** (sheet of paper)
FOE-llia DEE pah-PEH-oo

7) **livro** (book)
LEE-vroo

8) **caderno** (notebook)
kah-DEHR-noo

9) **cola** (glue)
KOH-lah

10) **tesoura** (scissors)
tee-ZO-rah

11) **lápis** (pencil)
LAH-peez

12) **borracha** (eraser)
boe-HAH-shah

13) **apontador** (pencil sharpener)
ah-pon-tah-DOHR

14) **caneta** (pen)
kah-NEA-tah

15) **canetinha** (marker)
kah-neah-CHEE-gna

16) **marca-texto** (highlighter)
MAHR-kah TEAZ-too

17) **envelope** (envelope)
en-veah-LAW-peah

18) **prancheta** (clipboard)
prun-SHEH-tah

19) **quadro-negro** (blackboard)
KWA-droo-NEAH-groo

20) **calculadora** (calculator)
cow-koo-lah-DOEH-rah

21) **régua** (ruler)
HEAH-gwa

22) **grampeador** (stapler)
grum-peah-ah-DOEHR

23) **estojo** (pouch/pencil case)
ez-TOE-zhoo

24) **carteira** (school desk)
kahr-TAY-rah

25) **mesa** (table)
MEAH-zah

26) **notebook** (laptop)
no-chee-BOO-kee

Este cálculo é muito complicado sem uma calculadora.
This calculation is too complicated without a calculator.

Use sua borracha para corrigir seu erro.
Use your eraser to correct your mistake.

Eu não consigo encontrar meu apontador.
I cannot find my pencil sharpener.

O ESCRITÓRIO (THE OFFICE)

1) **chefe** (boss)
   SHEH-fee

2) **superior** (superior)
   soo-peah-ree-OEHR

3) **funcionária** (employee)
   foon-see-oeh-NAH-ree-ah

4) **CEO/presidente** (CEO/president)
   C-E-O/preah-zee-DEN-chee

5) **sócio** (business partner)
   SAW-see-oo

6) **colega** (colleague)
   koeh-LEH-gah

7) **colega de trabalho** (co-worker)
   koeh-LEH-gah DEE trah-BAH-llio

8) **secretária** (secretary)
   seah-creah-TAH-ree-ah

9) **estação de trabalho** (cubicle)
   ez-tah-SUH-oo DEE trah-BAH-llio

10) **cadeira de escritório** (swivel chair)
    kah-DAY-rah DEE ez-cree-TOH-ree-oo

11) **mesa** (desk)
    MEAH-zah

12) **computador** (computer)
    kom-poo-tah-DOEHR

13) **impressora** (printer)
    eem-preah-SOEH-rah

14) **material de escritório** (office supplies)
    mah-teah-ree-OW DEE ez-cree-TOH-ree-oo

15) **carimbo** (rubber stamp)
    kah-REEM-boo

16) **porta-fita adesiva** (tape dispenser)
    POEHR-tah-FEE-tah ah-deah-ZEE-vah

17) **pasta** (folder)
    PAHZ-tah

18) **arquivo** (filing cabinet)
    ahr-KEE-voo

19) **fax** (fax)
    FAHKS

20) **telefone** (telephone)
    teah-leah-FOEH-nee

Eu realmente gosto do meu novo colega.
I really like my new colleague.

Dê seu número à minha secretária.
Give your number to my secretary.

Ninguém mais usa fax!
No one uses a fax anymore!

PROFISSÕES (PROFESSIONS/OCCUPATIONS)

1) **engenheiro** (engineer)
   en-zheah-GNAY-roo

2) **astronauta** (astronaut)
   ahz-troeh-NOW-tah

3) **piloto** (pilot)
   pee-LOEH-too

4) **juiz** (judge)
   zhoo-EEZ

5) **bombeiro** (firefighter)
   bom-BAY-roo

6) **policial** (police officer)
   poeh-lee-see-OW

7) **chef** (chef)
   CHEF

8) **condutor** (conductor)
   kon-doo-TOEHR

9) **professor** (professor)
   proeh-feah-SOEHR

10) **dançarina** (dancer)
    dun-sah-REE-nah

11) **empresário** (businessman)
    em-preah-ZAH-ree-oo

12) **adestrador de animais (**animal trainer)
    ah-deaz-trah-DOEHR DEE ah-nee-MAH-eez

Quando eu era criança, eu queria ser piloto.
When I was a kid, I wanted to be a pilot.

Ele se tornará um grande empresário.
He will become a good businessman.

Chame os bombeiros!
Call the firefighters!

MEIOS DE TRANSPORTE (TRANSPORTATION)

1) **bicicleta** (bike/bicycle)
   bee-see-KLEH-tah

2) **moto** (motorcycle/motorbike)
   MOH-too

3) **moto de neve** (snowmobile)
   MOH-too DEE NEH-vee

4) **carro** (car/automobile)
   KAH-hoo

5) **ônibus** (bus)
   OEH-nee-booz

6) **caminhão** (truck)
   kah-mee-GNUH-oo

7) **metrô** (subway)
   meah-TROEH

8) **trem** (train)
   TREM

9) **jet ski** (jet ski)
   zhetz-KEE

10) **barco** (boat)
    BAHR-koo

11) **navio de cruzeiro** (cruise ship)
    nah-VEE-oo DEE croo-ZAY-roo

12) **submarino** (submarine)
    soob-mah-REE-noo

13) **dirigível** (blimp/Zeppelin)
    dee-ree-ZHEE-veahl

14) **balão** (hot-air balloon)
    bah-LUH-oo

15) **avião** (plane/airplane)
    ah-vee-UH-oo

16) **helicóptero** (helicopter/chopper)
    eah-lee-KOEHP-teah-roo

17) **ônibus espacial** (space shuttle)
    OEH-nee-booz ez-pah-see-OW

Você vai de ônibus ou no seu carro?
Are you going to take the bus or your car?

Eu tenho medo de voar.
I am scared of flying.

Nós reservamos umas férias em um navio de cruzeiro.
We have booked a holiday on a cruise ship.

PAISAGENS (LANDSCAPES)

1) **montanha** (mountain)
   mon-TUH-gnah

2) **floresta tropical** (tropical rainforest)
   floeh-REZ-tah troeh-pee-COW

3) **deserto** (desert)
   deah-ZEAHR-too

4) **vulcão** (volcano)
   vool-KUH-oo

5) **penhasco** (cliff)
   peah-GNAHZ-koo

6) **praia** (beach)
   PRAH-yah

7) **floresta** (forest)
   floeh-REZ-tah

8) **caverna** (cave)
   kah-VEAHR-nah

9) **gêiser** (geyser)
   GHAY-zeahr

10) **cachoeira** (waterfall/falls)
    kah-shoeh-AY-rah

11) **rio** (river)
    HEE-oo

12) **ruínas** (ancient ruins)
    hoo-EE-nahz

Eu me perdi na floresta.
I got lost in the forest.

As melhores férias são passadas nas montanhas.
The best holidays are spent in the mountains.

Nós devemos cruzar o rio.
We must cross the river.

ESPORTES I (SPORTS I)

1) **arco e flecha** (archery)
   AHR-koo EAH FLEH-shah

2) **boxe** (boxing)
   BOX

3) **ciclismo** (cycling)
   see-KLEEZ-moo

4) **esgrima** (fencing)
   ez-GREE-mah

5) **futebol** (football/soccer)
   foo-chee-BALL

6) **rúgbi** (rugby)
   RUHG-bee

7) **pingue-pongue** (table tennis/ping-pong)
   PEEN-ghee-PON-ghee

8) **vôlei** (volleyball)
   VOEH-lay

9) **levantamento de peso** (weightlifting)
   leah-vun-tah-MEN-too DEE PEAH-zoo

10) **patinação** (skating)
    pah-chee-NAH-suh-oo

11) **esportes paralímpicos** (paralympic sports)
    ez-POEHR-teez pah-rah-LEEM-pee-kooz

12) **beisebol** (baseball)
    bay-zee-BALL

13) **basquete** (basketball)
    bahz-KEAH-chee

Eu realmente admiro os jogadores de rúgbi.
I really admire rugby players.

Eu vou à academia fazer levantamento de peso.
I go to the gym to do weightlifting.

Os franceses amam ciclismo.
French people love cycling.

ESPORTES II (SPORTS II)

1) **badminton** (badminton)
bed-MEEN-ton

2) **ginástica olímpica** (gymnastics)
zhee-NAHZ-tee-kah oh-LEEM-pee-kah

3) **remo** (rowing)
HEAH-moo

4) **escalada esportiva** (sport climbing)
ez-kah-LAH-dah ez-poehr-TEE-vah

5) **surfe** (surfing)
SOOR-fee

6) **tênis** (tennis)
TEAH-neez

7) **cama elástica** (trampoline)
KUH-mah eh-LAS-chee-kah

8) **luta livre** (wrestling)
LOO-tah LEE-vree

9) **esqui** (skiing)
ez-KEE

10) **esqueleto** (skeleton)
ez-keah-LEAH-too

11) **patinação artística** (figure skating)
pah-chee-nah-SUH-oo ahr-TEEZ-tee-kah

12) **natação** (swimming)
nah-tah-SUH-oo

13) **polo aquático** (water polo)
POH-loo ah-QUAH-tee-koo

14) **hóquei** (hockey)
HOH-key

O remo é muito popular na Inglaterra.
Rowing is very popular in England.

A Serena Williams é a melhor tenista de todas.
Serena Williams is the best tennis player.

Eu não sei as regras do polo aquático.
I do not know the rules of water polo.

DIA DE NATAL (CHRISTMAS DAY)

1) **visco** (mistletoe)
VEEZ-koo

2) **guirlanda** (garland)
geer-LUN-dah

3) **árvore de Natal** (Christmas tree)
AHR-voeh-ree DEE nah-TOW

4) **decoração de Natal** (Christmas decorations)
deah-koeh-rah-SUH-oo DEE nah-TOW

5) **presentes de Natal** (Christmas gifts/presents)
preah-ZEN-chees DEE nah-TOW

6) **ceia de Natal** (Christmas dinner)
SAY-ah DEE nah-TOW

7) **pirulito bengala** (candy cane)
pee-roo-LEE-too ben-GAH-lah

8) **biscoito de gengibre** (gingerbread man)
beez-KOEH-ee-too DEE zhen-ZHEE-bree

9) **elfo** (elf)
el-FOE

10) **chapéu de Natal** (Christmas hat)
shah-PEAH-oo DEE nah-TOW

11) **Papai Noel** (Santa Claus)
pah-PAH-ee no-EL

12) **trenó do Papai Noel** (Santa's sleigh)
treah-NAW doo pah-PAH-ee no-EL

13) **estrela de Natal** (Christmas star)
ez-TREAH-lah DEE nah-TOW

14) **boneco de neve** (snowman)
boeh-NEH-koo DEE NEH-vee

15) **velas** (candles)
VEH-laz

Nós comeremos salmão na ceia de Natal.
We will eat salmon for Christmas dinner.

O Papai Noel entra pela chaminé.
Santa Claus enters through the chimney.

Eu comprei uma árvore de Natal artificial.
I bought an artificial Christmas tree.

QUIZ #4

Use arrows to match the corresponding translations:

a. engineer

b. forest

c. wheelbarrow

d. mop

e. colleague

f. gardener

g. bike

h. cave

i. airplane

j. calculator

k. firefighter

l. beach

m. dirty laundry

n. bucket

o. rake

p. classroom

1. bombeiro

2. calculadora

3. sala de aula

4. roupa suja

5. balde

6. ancinho

7. floresta

8. avião

9. carrinho de mão

10. jardineiro

11. colega

12. bicicleta

13. esfregão

14. caverna

15. engenheiro

16. praia

Fill in the blank spaces with the options below (use each word only once):

Pedro é _____ de Engenharia Civil na Universidade de Delft. Ele está no terceiro ano. No futuro, ele quer ser _____ ou _____. Seu objetivo é ficar rico e viajar pelo mundo. Ele sonha em jogar _____ em uma _____ no Caribe. Ele também sonha em sair na água com seu próprio _____ ou com um _____. Seu _____ favorito é o Sr. Silva. Ele é muito inteligente e carismático. Pedro gostaria de seguir seus passos. No entanto, agora ele tem que ir à lavanderia para usar a _____ e lavar a _____. Para isso, ele deve primeiro ir ao supermercado comprar _____ e _____.

professor

sabão

vôlei

praia

amaciante de roupas

empresário

roupa suja

engenheiro

jet ski

máquina de lavar

aluno

barco

INSTRUMENTOS MUSICAIS (MUSICAL INSTRUMENTS)

1) **violão acústico** (acoustic guitar)
vee-oeh-LUH-oo ah-KOOZ-chee-koo

2) **guitarra elétrica** (electric guitar)
gee-TAH-hah eah-LEAH-tree-kah

3) **baixo** (bass guitar)
BYE-shoo

4) **bateria** (drums)
bah-teah-REE-ah

5) **piano** (piano)
pee-UH-noo

6) **trompete** (trumpet)
trom-PEH-chee

7) **harmônica** (harmonica)
ahr-MOEH-nee-kah

8) **flauta** (flute)
FLOU-tah

9) **clarinete** (clarinet)
klah-ree-NEAH-cheea

10) **harpa** (harp)
AHR-pah

11) **gaita de fole** (bagpipes)
GAH-ee-tah DEE FOH-lee

12) **violoncelo** (cello)
vee-oeh-lon-SEH-loo

13) **violino** (violin)
vee-oeh-LEE-noo

14) **saxofone** (saxophone)
sahk-soeh-FOEH-nee

Eu comecei a fazer aulas de piano.
I have started taking piano lessons.

A harpa é meu instrumento preferido.
The harp is my favorite instrument.

Jimi Hendrix foi um gênio da guitarra.
Jimi Hendrix was a guitar genius.

FRUTAS (FRUITS)

1) **morango** (strawberry)
moeh-RUN-goo

2) **mamão** (papaya)
mah-MUH-oo

3) **ameixa** (plum)
ah-MAY-shah

4) **melão** (melon)
meah-LUH-oo

5) **melancia** (watermelon)
meah-lun-SEE-ah

6) **banana** (banana)
bah-NAH-nah

7) **manga** (mango)
MUHN-gah

8) **pêssego** (peach)
PEAH-seah-goo

9) **framboesa** (raspberry)
frum-boeh-EAH-zah

10) **laranja** (orange)
lah-RUN-zhah

11) **limão siciliano** (lemon)
lee-MUH-oo see-see-lee-UH-noo

12) **abacaxi** (pineapple)
ah-bah-kah-SHEE

13) **limão** (lime)
lee-MUH-oo

14) **uvas** (grapes)
OO-vahz

15) **cereja** (cherry)
seah-REAH-zhah

16) **maçã** (apple)
mah-SUH

17) **pera** (pear)
PEAH-rah

18) **toranja** (grapefruit)
toeh-RUN-zhah

19) **graviola** (soursop)
grah-vee-OEH-lah

20) **coco** (coconut)
KOEH-koo

Eu queria um quilo de pera.
I would like a kilo of pears.

Ele come uma toranja no café da manhã.
He eats a grapefruit for breakfast.

Eu amo geleia de framboesa.
I love raspberry jam.

VEGETAIS (VEGETABLES)

1) **couve-flor** (cauliflower)
   ko-vee-FLOEHR

2) **aspargos** (asparagus)
   ahz-PAHR-gooz

3) **brócolis** (broccoli)
   BROH-koe-leez

4) **repolho** (cabbage)
   reah-POEH-llio

5) **alcachofra** (artichoke)
   ow-kah-SHOEH-frah

6) **couve-de-bruxelas** (Brussels sprouts)
   KO-vee DEE broo-SHEAH-luz

7) **milho** (corn)
   MEE-llio

8) **alface** (lettuce)
   ow-FAH-see

9) **espinafre** (spinach)
   ez-pee-NAH-free

10) **tomate** (tomato)
    toeh-MAH-chee

11) **pepino** (cucumber)
    peah-PEE-noo

12) **abobrinha** (zucchini)
    ah-boh-BREE-gnah

13) **cogumelo** (mushroom)
    koeh-goo-MEH-loo

14) **rúcula** (arugula)
    HOO-koo-lah

15) **beringela** (eggplant)
    beah-reen-ZHEH-lah

16) **pimentão** (bell pepper)
    pee-men-TUH-oo

17) **cebola** (onion)
    seah-BOEH-lah

18) **abóbora** (pumpkin/squash)
    ah-BOH-boh-rah

19) **batata** (potato)
    bah-TAH-tah

20) **acelga** (Swiss chard)
    ah-SELL-gah

Eu preparei uma sopa de repolho.
I prepared a cabbage soup.

Falta molho na salada de tomate.
The tomato salad lacks sauce.

Tem beringela na moussaka.
There are eggplants in the Moussaka.

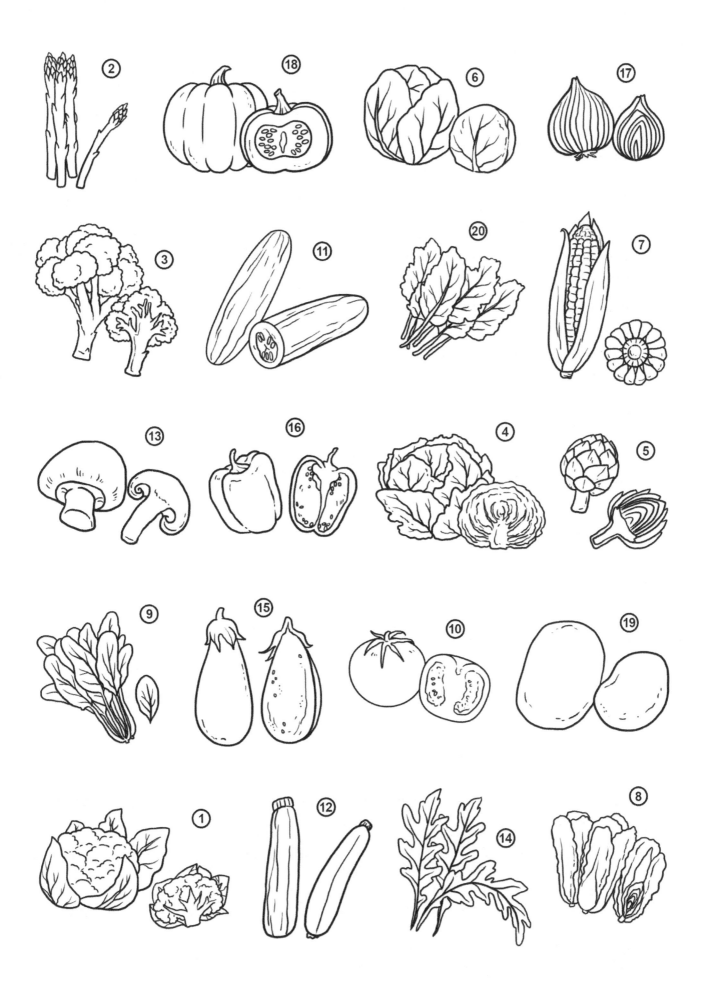

TECNOLOGIA (TECHNOLOGY)

1) **celular** (mobile)
   seah-loo-LAHR

2) **dispositivo** (device)
   deez-poeh-zee-CHEE-voo

3) **computador** (computer)
   com-poo-tah-DOEHR

4) **webcam** (web cam)
   web-KUM

5) **pen drive** (flash drive)
   pen DRY-vee

6) **disco rígido** (hard drive)
   DEEZ-koo HEE-zhee-doo

7) **cartão de memória** (memory card)
   kahr-TUH-oo DEE meah-MOH-ree-ah

8) **leitor de cartão** (card reader)
   lay-TOEHR DEE kahr-TUH-oo

9) **sem fio** (wireless)
   SEAHM FEE-oo

10) **painel solar** (solar panel)
    pah-ee-NELL soeh-LAHR

11) **impressora** (printer)
    eem-preah-SOEH-rah

12) **scanner** (scanner)
    SKUH-neahr

Eu tenho uma reunião pela webcam.
I have a meeting via webcam.

O cartão de memória da minha câmera está cheio.
My camera's memory card is full.

Eu vou salvar esses documentos no meu pen drive.
I am going to save these documents on my flash drive.

CIÊNCIAS (SCIENCE)

1) **laboratório** (laboratory)
   lah-boeh-rah-TOH-ree-oo

2) **pesquisador** (researcher)
   peahz-kee-zah-DOEHR

3) **cálculos** (calculations)
   COW-koo-looz

4) **cientista** (scientist)
   see-en-CHEEZ-tah

5) **jaleco** (lab coat)
   zhah-LEH-koo

6) **experimento** (experiment)
   ez-peah-ree-MEN-too

7) **equipamento de proteção pessoal** (personal protective equipment)
   eah-kee-pah-MEN-too DEE proeh-teah-SUH-oo peah-soeh-OW

8) **teste** (test)
   TEHZ-chee

9) **prêmio** (prize)
   PREAH-mee-oo

10) **risco** (risk)
    HEEZ-koo

11) **instrumento** (instrument)
    eenz-troo-MEN-too

12) **estatística** (statistics)
    ez-tah-TEEZ-tee-kah

O equipamento de proteção pessoal é obrigatório dentro do laboratório.
Personal protective equipment is mandatory in the laboratory.

Eu vim fazer um teste de COVID.
I have come for a COVID test.

Ele trabalha como cientista.
He works as a scientist.

ASTRONOMIA (ASTRONOMY)

1) **telescópio** (telescope)
teah-lez-KOEH-pee-oo

2) **sol** (sun)
SALL

3) **lua** (moon)
LOO-ah

4) **galáxia** (galaxy)
gah-LAH-ksee-ah

5) **cinturão de asteroides** (asteroid belt)
seen-too-RUH-oo DEE ahz-teah-
ROEH-ee-dez

6) **buraco negro** (black hole)
boo-RAH-koo NEAH-groo

7) **eclipse** (eclipse)
eah-CLEE-psee

8) **estrela cadente** (shooting star)
ez-TREAH-lah kah-DEN-chee

9) **estação espacial** (space station)
ez-tah-SUH-oo ez-pah-see-OW

10) **anã branca** (white dwarf)
ah-NUH BRUN-kah

11) **gigante vermelha** (red giant)
zhee-GUN-chee veahr-MEAH-llia

12) **órbita** (orbit)
OHR-bee-tah

13) **constelação** (constellation)
konz-teah-lah-SUH-oo

14) **energia escura** (dark energy)
eah-neahr-ZHEE-ah ez-KOO-rah

15) **Plutão** (Pluto)
ploo-TUH-oo

16) **nebulosa** (nebula)
neah-boo-LOEH-zah

17) **Mercúrio** (Mercury)
meahr-KOO-ree-oo

18) **Vênus** (Venus)
VEAH-nooz

19) **Terra** (Earth)
TEH-hah

20) **Marte** (Mars)
MAHR-chee

21) **Júpiter** (Jupiter)
ZHOOP-teahr

22) **Saturno** (Saturn)
sah-TOOHR-noo

23) **Urano** (Uranus)
oo-RUH-noo

24) **Netuno** (Neptune)
neah-TOO-noo

À noite, você pode ver a galáxia inteira.
At night, you can see the whole galaxy.

A estação espacial pousou em Marte.
The space station landed on Mars.

Uma anã branca é uma estrela pequena, porém brilhante.
A white dwarf is a small, but bright star.

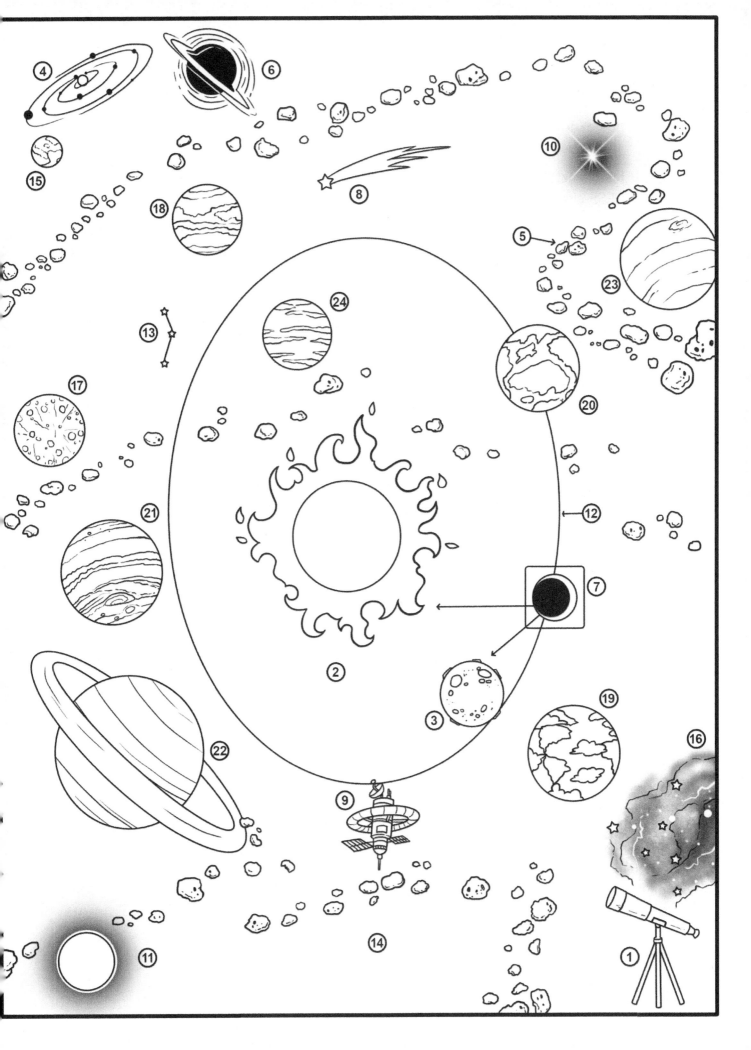

GEOGRAFIA (GEOGRAPHY)

1) **norte** (north)
NOR-chee

2) **leste** (east)
LESS-chee

3) **sul** (south)
SOOL

4) **oeste** (west)
oeh-ESS-chee

5) **Equador** (Equator)
eah-qua-DOEHR

6) **Trópico de Câncer** (Tropic of Cancer)
TROH-pee-koo DEE KUN-seahr

7) **Trópico de Capricórnio** (Tropic of Capricorn)
TROH-pee-koo DEE kah-pree-KOEHR-nee-oo

8) **Polo Sul** (South Pole)
POH-loo SOOL

9) **Polo Norte** (North Pole)
POH-loo NOR-chee

10) **Círculo Ártico** (Arctic Circle)
SEER-koo-loo AHR-chee-koo

11) **continente** (continent)
con-chee-NEN-chee

12) **no exterior** (overseas)
NOEH ez-teah-ree-OEHR

13) **África** (Africa)
AH-free-kah

14) **Ásia** (Asia)
AH-zee-ah

15) **América do Norte** (North America)
ah-MEH-ree-kah DOO NOR-chee

16) **América Central** (Central America)
ah-MEH-ree-kah cen-TROU

17) **América do Sul** (South America)
ah-MEH-ree-kah DOO SOOL

18) **Europa** (Europe)
eah-oo-ROH-pah

19) **Oceania** (Oceania)
oeh-ceah-uh-NEE-ah

20) **Antártica** (Antarctica)
un-TAHR-chee-kah

21) **meridiano** (meridian)
meah-ree-dee-UH-noo

22) **paralelo** (parallel)
pah-rah-LEAH-loo

23) **Oceano Atlântico** (Atlantic Ocean)
oeh-ceah-UH-noo ah-TLUN-chee-koo

24) **Oceano Pacífico** (Pacific Ocean)
oeh-ceah-UH-noo pah-SEE-fee-koo

Eu moro no sul da França.
I live in the south of France.

Eu amo surfar no Oceano Atlântico.
I love to surf in the Atlantic Ocean.

Nós planejamos uma viagem para a Europa.
We have planned a trip to Europe.

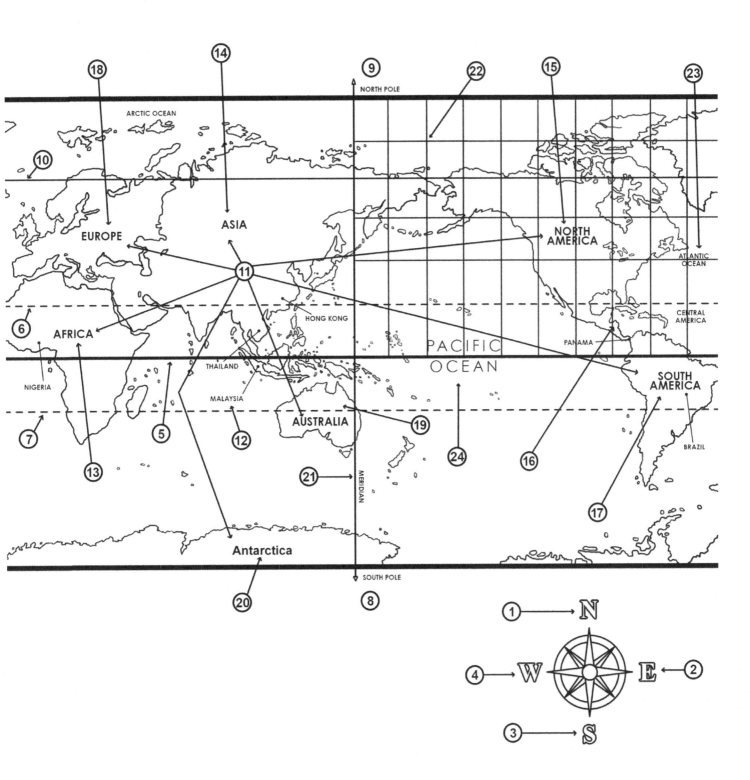

O HOSPITAL (THE HOSPITAL)

1) **médico** (doctor/general practitioner)
MEH-dee-koo

2) **enfermeira** (nurse)
en-feahr-MAY-rah

3) **ambulância** (ambulance)
um-boo-LUN-see-ah

4) **kit de primeiros socorros** (first-aid kit)
KEET DEE pree-MAY-rooz soeh-KOH-hooz

5) **termômetro** (thermometer)
teahr-MOEH-meah-troo

6) **maca** (stretcher)
MAH-kah

7) **seringa** (syringe)
see-REEN-gah

8) **agulha** (needle)
ah-GOO-llia

9) **estetoscópio** (stethoscope)
ez-teah-toz-KOH-pee-oo

10) **muletas** (crutches)
moo-LEAH-tahz

11) **cadeira de rodas** (wheelchair)
kah-DAY-rah DEE HOH-dahz

12) **sala de observação** (observation room)
SAH-lah DEE ob-seahr-vah-SUH-oo

13) **cama de hospital** (hospital bed)
KUH-mah DEE oz-pee-TOW

14) **injeção** (injection)
een-zheah-SUH-oo

15) **cirurgia** (surgery)
see-ROOHR-ZHEE-ah

16) **histórico médico** (medical history)
eez-TOH-ree-koo MEH-dee-koo

17) **paciente** (patient)
pah-see-EN-chee

18) **comprimido** (pill/tablet)
com-pree-MEE-doo

Eu tenho uma consulta com o médico na quarta-feira.
I have an appointment with the doctor on Wednesday.

A cama do hospital é desconfortável.
This hospital bed is uncomfortable.

Minha filha quer ser enfermeira.
My daughter wants to become a nurse.

113

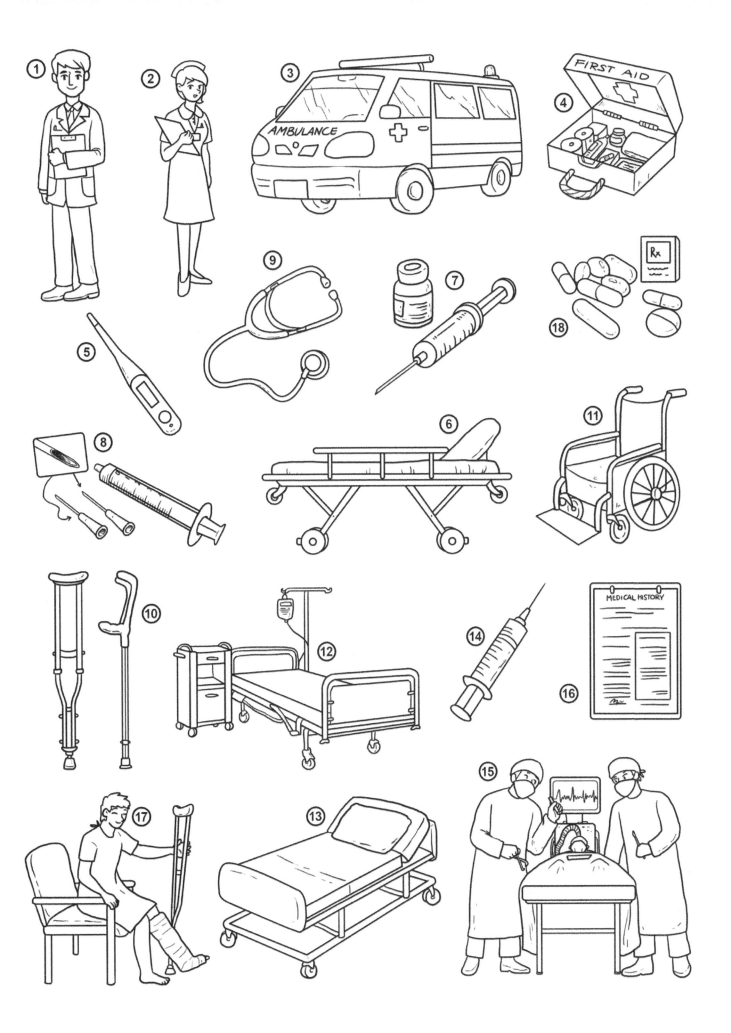

A FAZENDA (THE FARM)

1) **celeiro** (barn)
seah-LAY-roo

2) **estábulo** (cowshed/stable)
ez-TAH-boo-loo

3) **fazendeiro** (farmer)
fah-zen-DAY-roo

4) **arado** (plough)
ah-RAH-doo

5) **silo** (silo)
SEE-loo

6) **moinho** (mill)
moeh-EE-gno

7) **cocho de água** (water trough)
KOEH-sho DEE AH-gwa

8) **galinheiro** (henhouse)
gah-lee-GNAY-roo

9) **colmeia** (beehive)
koul-MEH-ee-ah

10) **fardo de feno** (hay bale)
FAHR-doo DEE FEAH-noo

11) **gado** (cattle)
GAH-doo

12) **ordenhar** (to milk)
oehr-deah-GNAHR

13) **rebanho** (herd/flock)
reah-BUH-gnoo

14) **galinha** (hen)
gah-LEE-gnah

15) **poço** (well)
POEH-soo

16) **sistema de irrigação** (irrigation system)
sis-TEAH-mah DEE ee-hee-gah-SUH-oo

17) **espantalho** (scarecrow)
ez-pun-TAH-llio

18) **estrada de terra** (dirt road)
ez-TRAH-dah DEE TEH-hah

Minhas galinhas põem uma dúzia de ovos por dia.
My hens lay a dozen eggs per day.

Eu coloquei um espantalho no meu campo para espantar os pássaros.
I installed a scarecrow in my field to scare birds away.

Vire à esquerda e siga a estrada de terra.
Turn left and follow the dirt road.

QUIZ #5

Use arrows to match the corresponding translations:

a. laboratory

b. pear

c. researcher

d. north

e. well

f. bagpipes

g. wheelchair

h. henhouse

i. eggplant

j. nurse

k. Earth

l. cauliflower

m. strawberry

n. device

o. statistics

p. cherry

1. dispositivo

2. cadeira de rodas

3. pera

4. couve-flor

5. morango

6. Terra

7. laboratório

8. enfermeira

9. cereja

10. estatística

11. gaita de fole

12. poço

13. norte

14. beringela

15. pesquisador

16. galinheiro

Fill in the blank spaces with the options below (use each word only once):

Meus avós moram na _____, no _____ do Brasil. Eu decidi visitá-los no próximo mês. Não nos vemos com muita frequência porque moro em Nova York, mas graças ao meu _____ e _____, mantemos contato. Minha avó é uma excelente tocadora de _____. Ela costumava tocar em bares da cidade. Ela me ensinou a tocar _____! Meu avô é _____. Ele planta _____. Ele faz os bolos mais deliciosos do mundo com _____ e _____.

computador	piano
repolho	maçãs
América do Sul	fazendeiro
guitarra elétrica	webcam
framboesas	norte

COMIDA (FOOD)

1) **uvas passas** (raisins)
   OO-vahz PAH-sahz

2) **castanhas** (nuts)
   kahz-TUH-gnahz

3) **carne** (meat)
   KAHR-nee

4) **cordeiro** (lamb)
   koehr-DAY-roo

5) **peixe** (fish)
   PAY-shee

6) **frango** (chicken)
   FRUN-goo

7) **peru** (turkey)
   peah-ROO

8) **mel** (honey)
   MELL

9) **açúcar** (sugar)
   ah-SOO-kahr

10) **sal** (salt)
    SAWL

11) **pimenta** (pepper)
    pee-MEN-tah

12) **bacon** (bacon)
    BAY-com

13) **linguiça** (sausage)
    leen-GWEE-sah

14) **ketchup** (ketchup)
    KET-shoop

15) **maionese** (mayonnaise)
    mah-ee-oeh-NEH-zee

16) **mostarda** (mustard)
    moehz-TAHR-dah

17) **geleia** (jam)
    zheah-LEH-ee-ah

18) **manteiga** (butter)
    mun-TAY-gah

19) **suco** (juice)
    SOO-koo

20) **leite** (milk)
    LAY-chee

Eu não consigo comer batata frita sem maionese.
I cannot eat fries without mayonnaise.

Abelhas produzem mel.
Bees make honey.

Você prefere frango ou peixe?
Do you prefer chicken or fish?

PRATOS (DISHES)

1) **lasanha** (lasagna)
lah-ZUN-gnah

2) **omelete de batata** (potato omelette)
oeh-meah-LEH-chee DEE bah-TAH-tah

3) **bolo de carne** (meatloaf)
BOEH-loo DEE KAHR-nee

4) **macarrão frito** (fried noodles)
mah-kah-HUH-oo FREE-too

5) **macarrão com queijo** (macaroni and cheese)
mah-kah-HUH-oo KOM KAY-zhoo

6) **paella** (paella)
pah-EAH-llia

7) **costela ao barbecue** (barbecued ribs)
koz-TEAH-lah OW bahr-bee-KILL

8) **broa de milho** (cornbread)
BRO-AH DEE MEE-llio

9) **rolinho primavera** (spring roll)
hoeh-LEE-gnoo pree-mah-VEAH-rah

10) **x-burguer** (cheeseburger)
sheez-BOOR-geahr

11) **frango frito** (fried chicken)
FRUN-goo FREE-too

12) **salada Caesar** (Caesar salad)
sah-LAH-dah SEE-zahr

13) **sopa de cebola** (onion soup)
SOEH-pah DEE ceah-BOEH-lah

14) **salada de repolho** (coleslaw)
sah-LAH-dah DEE heah-POEH-llio

15) **asa de frango picante** (spicy chicken wings)
AH-zah DEE FRUN-goo pee-KUN-chee

16) **cookies de chocolate** (chocolate-chip cookies)
KOO-keez DEE shoeh-koeh-LAH-chee

17) **torta de limão** (key lime pie)
TOHR-tah DEE lee-MUH-oo

18) **cheesecake** (cheesecake)
chee-zee-KAY-kee

Os americanos amam macarrão com queijo.
Americans love macaroni and cheese.

Eu vou pedir sopa de cebola.
I am going to order onion soup.

Cheesecake é a minha sobremesa preferida.
Cheesecake is my favorite dessert.

121

FRUTOS DO MAR (SEAFOOD)

1) **anchovas** (anchovy)
   un-SHOEH-vahz

2) **bacalhau** (cod)
   bah-kah-LLIOW

3) **caranguejo-aranha** (spider crab)
   kah-run-GEAH-zhoo ah-ruh-GNAH

4) **cavalinha** (mackerel)
   kah-vah-LEE-gnah

5) **lagosta** (lobster)
   lah-GOZ-tah

6) **vieira** (scallop)
   vee-AY-rah

7) **pargo** (snapper)
   PAHR-goo

8) **ovas de salmão** (salmon roe)
   OH-vahz DEE saw-MUH-oo

9) **caranguejo** (crab)
   kah-run-GEAH-zhoo

10) **marisco** (shellfish)
    mah-REEZ-koo

11) **enguia** (eel)
    en-GEE-ah

12) **camarão** (shrimp)
    kah-mah-RUH-oo

Eu quero anchovas na minha pizza.
I want anchovies on my pizza.

Vieiras são muito caras.
Scallops are very expensive.

Eu comprei salmão escocês para o jantar.
I bought Scottish salmon for dinner.

FORMAS (SHAPES)

1) **círculo** (circle)
   SEEHR-koo-loo

2) **oval** (oval)
   oeh-VOW

3) **triângulo** (triangle)
   tree-UN-goo-loo

4) **retângulo** (rectangle)
   heah-TUN-goo-loo

5) **quadrado** (square)
   kwah-DRAH-doo

6) **trapézio** (trapezoid)
   trah-PEAH-zee-oo

7) **losango** (rhombus)
   loeh-ZUN-goo

8) **cubo** (cube)
   KOO-boo

9) **pentágono** (pentagon)
   pen-TAH-goeh-noo

10) **hexágono** (hexagon)
   eah-KZAH-goeh-noo

11) **seta** (arrow)
   CEH-tah

12) **cruz** (cross)
   KROOZ

13) **coração** (heart)
   koeh-rah-SUH-oo

14) **estrela** (star)
   ez-TREAH-lah

15) **cilindro** (cylinder)
   see-LEEN-droo

16) **cone** (cone)
   KOEH-nee

17) **pirâmide** (pyramid)
   pee-RUH-mee-dee

18) **esfera** (sphere)
   ez-FEH-rah

19) **prisma** (prism)
   PREEZ-mah

Você visitou a pirâmide do Louvre?
Have you visited the Louvre pyramid?

Meu bebê ama brincar com cubos.
My baby loves to play with cubes.

Todo quadrado é, certamente, também um retângulo.
Every square is of course also a rectangle.

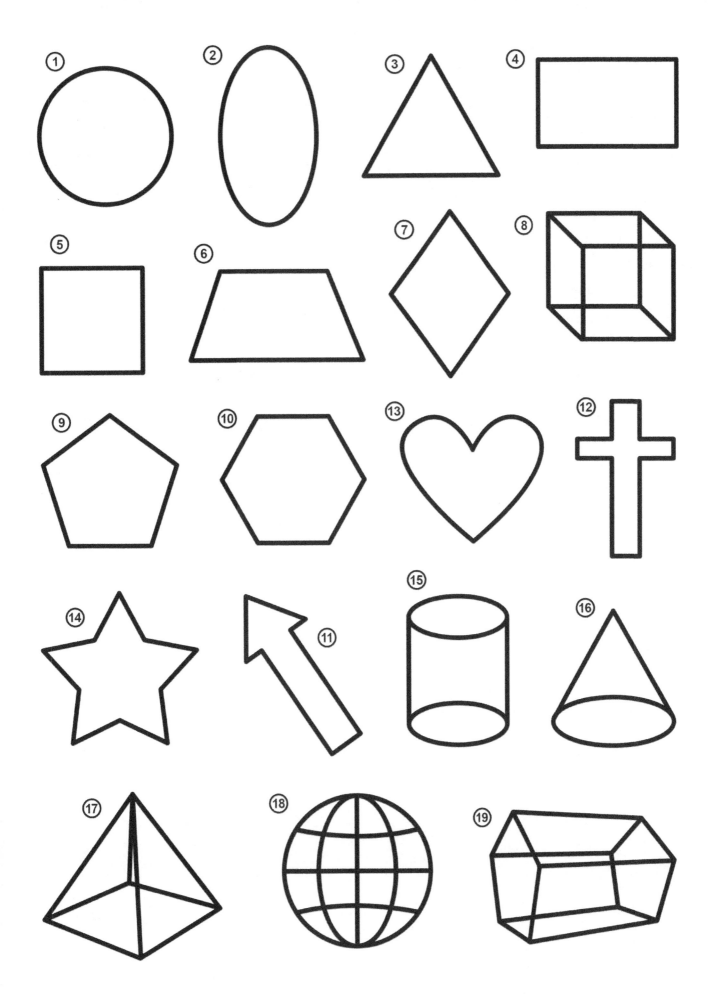

O SUPERMERCADO (THE SUPERMARKET)

1) **carrinho** (shopping cart)
   kah-HEE-gnoo

2) **armário/vitrine** (cabinet/display case)
   ahr-MAH-ree-oo/vee-TREE-nee

3) **cliente** (customer)
   klee-EN-chee

4) **caixa** (cashier)
   KAH-ee-shah

5) **nota fiscal** (receipt)
   NOH-tah FEES-kahl

6) **padaria** (bakery)
   pah-dah-REE-ah

7) **frutas e vegetais** (fruits and vegetables)
   FROO-tahz EAH veah-zheah-TAH-eez

8) **carne** (meat)
   KAHR-nee

9) **laticínios** (dairy products)
   lah-chee-SEE-nee-ooz

10) **peixe** (fish)
    PAY-shee

11) **comida congelada** (frozen food)
    koeh-MEE-dah kon-zheah-LAH-dah

12) **frango** (chicken)
    FRUN-goo

13) **legumes** (legumes)
    leah-GOO-meahz

14) **lanches** (snacks)
    LUN-sheez

15) **sobremesa** (dessert)
    soeh-breah-MEAH-zah

16) **bebidas** (drinks)
    beah-BEE-dahz

17) **artigos para o lar** (household items)
    ahr-CHEE-gooz PAH-rah OO LAHR

18) **esteira** (conveyor belt)
    ez-TAY-rah

Eu compro meu pão na padaria todos os dias.
I get my bread at the bakery every morning.

Sou vegetariano, não como carne.
I am a vegetarian; I do not eat meat.

Esta loja tem uma grande seleção de frutas e vegetais.
This shop has a great selection of fruits and vegetables.

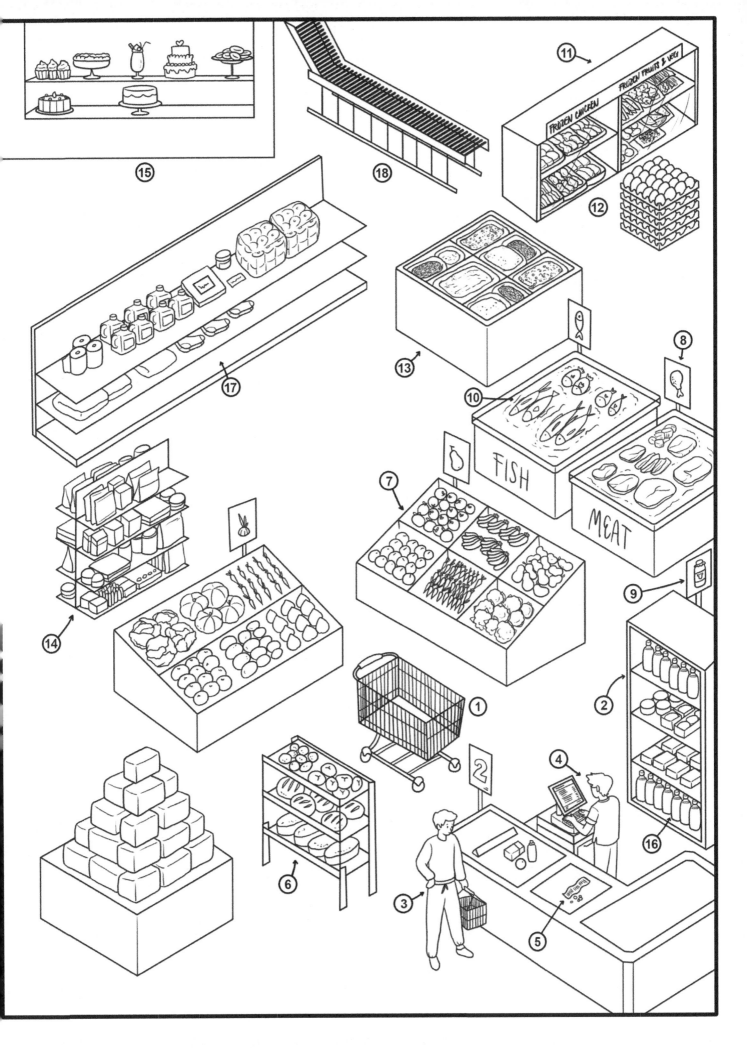

MÍDIA (MEDIA)

1) **revista** (magazine)
   heah-VEEZ-tah

2) **fax** (fax)
   FAHX

3) **jornal** (newspaper)
   zhoehr-NOW

4) **correio postal** (postal mail)
   koeh-HAY-oo poz-TOW

5) **carta** (letter)
   KAHR-tah

6) **rádio** (radio)
   HAH-dee-oo

7) **gibi** (comic)
   zhee-BEE

8) **livro** (book)
   LEE-vroo

9) **fotografia** (photography)
   foeh-toeh-grah-FEE-ah

10) **telefone fixo** (landline phone)
    teah-leah-FOEH-nee FEEK-soo

11) **TV** (TV)
    TEAH-veah

12) **filme** (movie)
    FEW-mee

13) **celular** (mobile phone/cell phone)
    ce-loo-LAHR

14) **língua de sinais** (sign language)
    LEEN-gwah DEE see-NAH-eez

O show da Beyoncé vai ao ar na TV amanhã.
Beyoncé's concert airs on TV tomorrow night.

Você pode me dar o número do seu celular?
Can you give me your cell number?

Eu mandei uma carta para ele.
I have sent him a letter.

A FEIRA/O PARQUE DE DIVERSÕES (THE FAIR/THE AMUSEMENT PARK)

1) **casa de espelhos** (house of mirrors)
KAH-zah DEE ez-PEAH-llioz

2) **barca** (pirate ship/boat swing)
BAHR-kah

3) **bilheteria** (ticket booth)
bee-llieah-teah-REE-ah

4) **cadeira voadora** (swing ride)
kah-DAY-rah voeh-ah-DOEH-rah

5) **montanha-russa** (roller coaster)
mon-TUH-gna HOO-sah

6) **roda-gigante** (Ferris wheel)
HOH-dah-zhee-GUN-chee

7) **carrossel** (carousel/merry-go-round)
kah-hoeh-SELL

8) **carrinho bate-bate** (bumper cars)
kah-HEE-gnoo bah-chee-BAH-chee

9) **xícara maluca** (teacups/cup and saucer)
SHEE-kah-rah mah-LOO-kah

10) **pêndulo** (pendulum)
PEN-doo-loo

11) **fliperama** (arcade room)
flee-peah-RUH-mah

12) **salsicha empanada** (corn dog)
saw-SEE-shah em-pah-NAH-dah

13) **raspadinha** (snow cone)
hahz-pah-DEE-gnah

14) **algodão doce** (cotton candy)
ow-goo-DUH-oo DOEH-see

15) **maçã do amor** (candy apple)
mah-SUH DOO ah-MOEHR

Eu amo montanhas-russas.
I love roller coasters.

Ele se perdeu na casa de espelhos.
He got lost in the house of mirrors.

Eu comi algodão doce demais.
I ate too much cotton candy.

EVENTOS DA VIDA (LIFE EVENTS)

1) **nascimento** (birth)
nah-see-MEN-too

2) **batismo** (christening/baptism)
bah-CHEEZ-moo

3) **primeiro dia de aula** (first day of school)
pree-MAY-roo DEE-ah DEE OW-lah

4) **fazer amigos** (make friends)
fah-ZEAHR ah-MEE-gooz

5) **aniversário** (birthday)
ah-nee-veahr-SAH-ree-oo

6) **se apaixonar** (fall in love)
SEE ah-pah-ee-SHOEH-nahr

7) **formatura** (graduation)
foehr-mah-TOO-rah

8) **começar a universidade** (to start university/begin college)
koeh-meah-SAHR AH oo-nee-veahr-see-DAH-dee

9) **conseguir um emprego** (get a job)
kon-ce-GEER OOM em-PREAH-goo

10) **virar um empreendedor** (become an entrepreneur)
vee-RAHR OMM em-preah-en-deah-DOEHR

11) **viajar o mundo** (travel around the world)
vee-ah-ZHAHR oeh MOON-doo

12) **se casar** (get married)
SEE kah-ZAHR

13) **ter um filho** (have a baby)
TEAHR OOM FEE-llio

14) **comemorar um aniversário** (celebrate a birthday)
koeh-mea-moeh-RAHR OOM ah-nee-veahr-SAH-ree-oo

15) **aposentadoria** (retirement)
ah-poeh-zen-tah-doeh-REE-ah

16) **morte** (death)
MOR-chee

Eu me caso mês que vem.
I am getting married next month.

Meus pais são aposentados.
My parents are retired.

Gabrielle finalmente encontrou um emprego.
Gabrielle has finally found a job.

ADJETIVOS I (ADJECTIVES I)

1) **grande** (big)
GRUN-dee

2) **pequeno/a** (small)
peah-KEAH-noo/nah

3) **barulhento/a** (loud)
bah-roo-LLIEN-too/tah

4) **silencioso/a** (silent)
see-len-see-OEH-zoo/zah

5) **longo/a** (long)
LON-goo/gah

6) **curto/a** (short)
KOOHR-too/tah

7) **largo/a** (wide)
LAHR-goo/gah

8) **estreito/a** (narrow)
ez-TRAY-too/tah

9) **caro/a** (expensive)
KAH-roo/rah

10) **barato/a** (cheap)
bah-RAH-too/tah

11) **rápido/a** (fast)
HAH-pee-doo/dah

12) **devagar** (slow)
dee-vah-GAHR

13) **vazio/a** (empty)
vah-ZEE-oo/ah

14) **cheio/a** (full)
SHAY-oo/ah

15) **macio/a** (soft)
mah-SEE-oo/ah

16) **duro/a** (hard)
DOO-roo/rah

17) **alto/a** (tall)
OW-too/tah

18) **baixo/a** (short)
BYE-shoo/shah

O cachorro do vizinho é muito barulhento.
The neighbor's dog is very loud.

Este restaurante é bom e barato.
This restaurant is good and cheap.

O guepardo é o animal mais rápido.
The cheetah is the fastest animal.

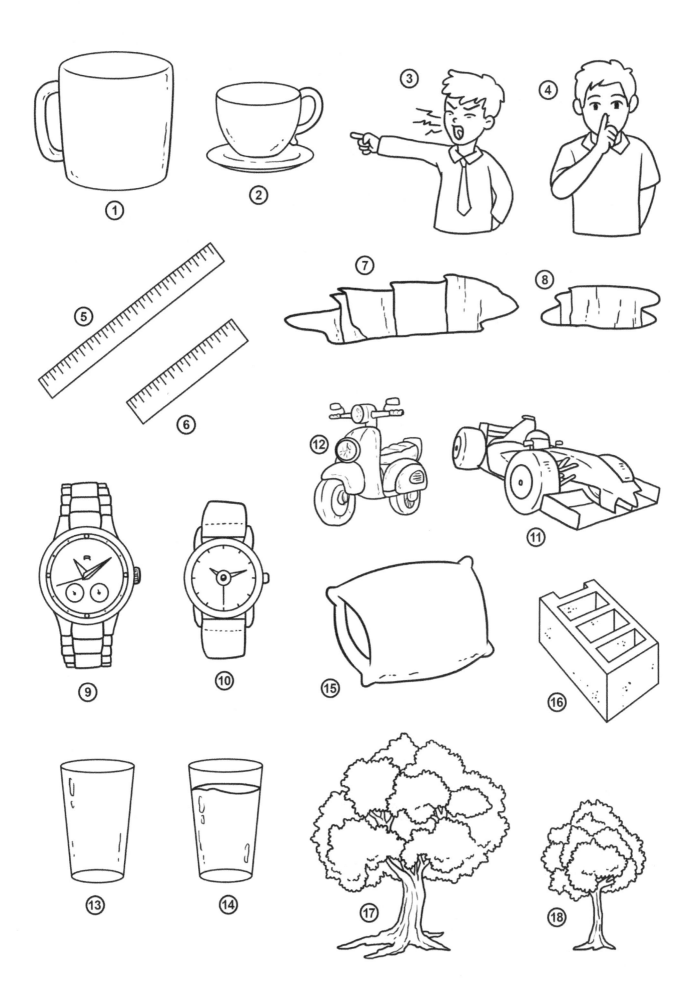

QUIZ #6

Use arrows to match the corresponding translations:

a. book

b. dairy products

c. roller coaster

d. eel

e. empty

f. birthday

g. letter

h. cotton candy

i. carousel

j. turkey

k. drinks

l. cross

m. nuts

n. fish

o. onion soup

p. arrow

1. bebidas

2. enguia

3. castanhas

4. peixe

5. sopa de cebola

6. peru

7. laticínios

8. cruz

9. montanha-russa

10. seta

11. livro

12. carta

13. algodão doce

14. aniversário

15. vazio

16. carrossel

Fill in the blank spaces with the options below (use each word only once):

Paula e suas amigas fizeram um delicioso jantar para comemorar o _____ de Joana. Em setembro, todas elas vão _____. Paula só vai estudar no ano que vem, porque ela quer _____ primeiro. A comida não era _____, mas o jantar valeu a pena. Estava uma delícia. Como aperitivo havia _____ e _____. Pauline ficou feliz porque gosta de frutos do mar. Depois veio o prato principal. Elas poderiam escolher entre _____ e _____ com _____. Pauline optou pelo frango, mas infelizmente estava _____ e um pouco queimado, e as demais acharam a lasanha com muito _____. Como _____, elas desfrutaram de um delicioso fondant de chocolate.

batata   sobremesa

duro   lasanha

aniversário   caranguejo

barata   frango

sal   começar a universidade

vieiras   viajar o mundo

ADJETIVOS II (ADJECTIVES II)

1) **novo/a** (new)
NOEH-voo/vah

2) **velho/a** (old)
VEH-llio/lliah

3) **confortável** (comfortable)
con-foehr-TAH-veah-oo

4) **desconfortável** (uncomfortable)
deahz-con-foehr-TAH-veah-oo

5) **perigoso/a** (dangerous)
peah-ree-GOEH-zoo/zah

6) **irritante** (annoying)
ee-hee-TUN-chee

7) **trêmulo** (shaky)
TREAH-moo-loo

8) **completo/a** (complete)
com-PLEH-too/tah

9) **incomplete/a** (incomplete)
een-com-PLEH-too/tah

10) **quebrado/a** (broken)
keah-BRAH-doo/dah

11) **lindo/a** (gorgeous)
LEEN-doo/dah

12) **virtuoso/a** (virtuous)
veer-too-OEH-zoo/zah

13) **similar** (similar)
see-mee-LAHR

14) **diferente** (different)
dee-feah-REN-chee

15) **aberto/a** (open)
ah-BEAR-too/tah

16) **fechado/a** (closed)
feah-SHAH-doo/dah

Aqueles gêmeos são muito similares.
Those twins are very similar.

Meu sofá é velho, mas confortável.
My sofa is old but comfortable.

Essa loja nunca está aberta!
This shop is never open!

ADVÉRBIOS (ADVERBS)

1) **aqui** (here)
ah-KEE

2) **lá** (there)
LAH

3) **perto** (near)
PEAR-too

4) **longe** (far)
LON-zhee

5) **para cima** (up)
PAH-rah SEE-mah

6) **para baixo** (down)
PAH-rah BAH-ee-shoo

7) **dentro** (inside)
DEN-troo

8) **fora** (outside)
FOH-rah

9) **à frente** (ahead)
AH FREN-chee

10) **atrás** (behind)
AH-TRAHZ

11) **não** (no)
NUH-oo

12) **sim** (yes)
SYM

13) **agora** (now)
ah-GOH-rah

14) **bem/bom/certo** (well/good/right)
BEM/BOM/SEHR-too

15) **ruim/errado** (bad/wrong)
hoo-YM/eah-HAH-doo

Estou te esperando lá dentro.
I am waiting for you inside.

Me ligue agora.
Call me now.

Vamos comer aqui ou lá?
Are we eating here or over there?

DIREÇÕES (DIRECTIONS)

1) **quarteirão** (block)
   kwahr-tay-RUH-oo

2) **praça** (square)
   PRAH-sah

3) **parque** (park)
   PAHR-keah

4) **metrô** (subway)
   meah-TROEH

5) **esquina** (corner)
   ez-KEE-nah

6) **avenida** (avenue)
   ah-veah-NEE-dah

7) **rua** (street)
   HOO-ah

8) **ponto de ônibus** (bus stop)
   PON-too DEE OEH-nee-booz

9) **semáforo** (traffic lights)
   seah-MAH-foeh-roo

10) **faixa de pedestres**
    (crossing/crosswalk)
    FAH-ee-shah DEE peah-DEAHZ-trees

11) **para frente** (forward)
    PAH-rah FREN-chee

12) **para trás** (backward)
    PAH-rah TRAHZ

13) **esquerda** (left)
    ez-KEAHR-dah

14) **direita** (right)
    dee-RAY-tah

15) **placas de trânsito** (road signs)
    PLAH-kaz DEE TRUN-zee-too

16) **guarda de trânsito** (traffic police)
    GWAR-dah DEE TRUN-zee-too

Eu não gosto do cheiro do metrô.
I do not like the smell in the subway.

Pegue a segunda rua à esquerda.
Take the second street on the left.

Você deve usar a faixa de pedestres.
You must use the crosswalk.

O RESTAURANTE (THE RESTAURANT)

1) **gerente** (manager)
   zheah-REN-chee

2) **mesa** (table)
   MEAH-zah

3) **cardápio** (menu)
   kahr-DAH-pee-oo

4) **prato** (dish)
   PRAH-too

5) **aperitivo** (appetizer)
   ah-peah-REE-tee-voo

6) **entrada** (starter)
   en-TRAH-dah

7) **prato principal** (main course)
   PRAH-too preen-SEE-pow

8) **sobremesa** (dessert)
   soeh-breah-MEAH-zah

9) **jantar** (dinner)
   zhun-TAHR

10) **cozinheiro** (cook)
    koeh-zee-GNAY-roo

11) **garçom** (waiter)
    gahr-SOM

12) **garçonete** (waitress)
    gahr-soeh-NEH-chee

13) **gorjeta** (tip)
    goer-ZHEAH-tah

14) **cadeira alta** (high chair)
    kah-DAY-rah OW-tah

15) **carta de vinhos** (wine list)
    KAHR-tah DEE VEE-gnoos

16) **confeiteiro** (pastry chef)
    kon-fay-TAY-roo

Você gostaria de ver nosso cardápio?
Would you like to see our menu?

Eu quero um aperitivo, por favor.
I will have an appetizer please.

Parabenize seu cozinheiro!
Congratulate your cook!

O SHOPPING (THE MALL)

1) **piso/andar** (floor/story)
   PEE-zoo/un-DAHR

2) **aquário** (aquarium)
   ah-KWA-ree-oo

3) **praça de alimentação** (food court)
   PRAH-sah DEE ah-lee-men-tah-SUH-
   oo

4) **elevador** (elevator)
   eah-leah-vah-DOEHR

5) **escada rolante** (escalators)
   ez-KAH-dah hoeh-LUN-chee

6) **saída de emergência** (emergency exit)
   sah-EE-dah DEE eah-mer-ZHEN-see-a

7) **salão de beleza** (beauty salon)
   sah-LUH-oo DEE beah-LEAH-zah

8) **loja de roupas** (clothing store)
   LAW-zhah DEE HO-pahs

9) **playground** (playground)
   play-GROUND

10) **segurança** (security guard)
    seah-goo-RUN-sah

11) **câmera de vigilância** (surveillance camera)
    KUH-meah-rah DEE vee-zhee-LUN-
    see-ah

12) **padaria** (bakery)
    pah-dah-REE-ah

13) **loja de artigos esportivos** (sports store)
    LAW-zhah DEE ahr-CHEE-goos ez-
    poehr-CHEE-voohs

14) **fonte** (fountain)
    fon-CHEE

Pegue o elevador e pare no segundo piso.
Take the elevator and stop on the second floor.

Eu vou levar meu filho para o playground.
I am going to take my son to the playground.

Eu moro ao lado da loja de artigos esportivos.
I live next to the sports store.

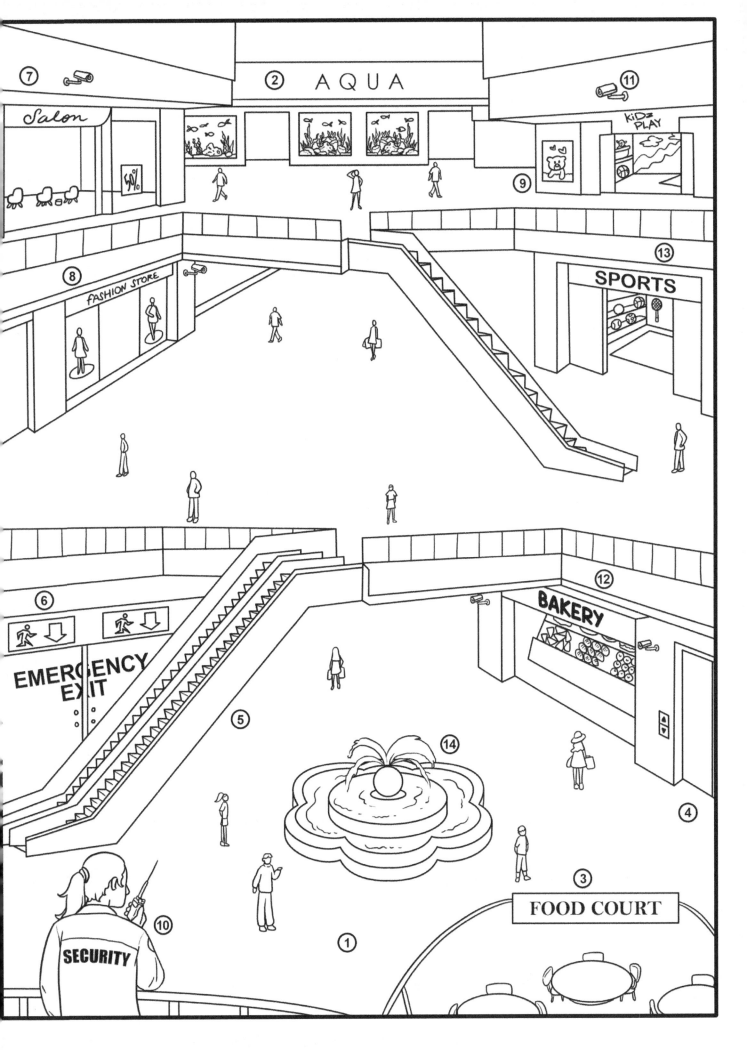

VERBOS I (VERBS I)

1) **conversar** (to talk)
   con-VEAHR-sahr

2) **beber** (to drink)
   beah-BEAHR

3) **comer** (to eat)
   koeh-MEAHR

4) **andar** (to walk)
   un-DAHR

5) **abrir** (to open)
   ah-BREEHR

6) **fechar** (to close)
   feah-SHAHR

7) **dar** (to give)
   DAHR

8) **ver** (to see)
   VEAHR

9) **seguir** (to follow)
   seah-GEER

10) **abraçar** (to hug)
    ah-brah-SAHR

11) **beijar** (to kiss)
    bay-ZHAR

12) **comprar** (to buy)
    com-PRAHR

13) **ouvir** (to listen)
    o-VEER

14) **cantar** (to sing)
    kun-TAHR

15) **dançar** (to dance)
    dun-SAHR

Você tem que fechar a janela.
You must close the window.

Me siga!
Follow me!

Eu dei 10 euros a ele.
I gave him 10 euros.

VERBOS II (VERBS II)

1) **escrever** (to write)
   ez-kreah-VEAHR

2) **ler** (to read)
   LEAHR

3) **limpar** (to clean)
   leem-PAHR

4) **pegar** (to pick up)
   peah-GAHR

5) **encontrar** (to find)
   en-con-TRAHR

6) **lavar** (to wash)
   lah-VAHR

7) **assistir** (to watch)
   ah-sis-TEER

8) **consertar** (to fix)
   con-seahr-TAHR

9) **pensar** (to think)
   pen-SAHR

10) **levar** (to take)
    leah-VAHR

11) **cortar** (to cut)
    koer-TAHR

12) **parar** (to stop)
    pah-RAHR

13) **chorar** (to cry)
    shoeh-RAHR

14) **sorrir** (to smile)
    soeh-HEER

15) **ajudar** (to help)
    ah-zhoo-DAHR

Pare de chorar.
Stop crying.

Eu vou limpar meu apartamento.
I am going to clean my flat.

Eu consertei o motor do meu carro.
I have repaired my car's engine.

CONSTRUÇÃO I (CONSTRUCTION I)

1) **guindaste** (crane)
geen-DAHZ-chee

2) **fita de isolamento** (hazard tape)
FEE-tah DEE ee-zoeh-lah-MEN-too

3) **cone de trânsito** (traffic cone)
KOEH-nee DEE TRUN-zee-too

4) **pá** (construction shovel)
PAH

5) **martelo** (hammer)
mahr-TEH-loo

6) **cortador de fio** (wire cutters)
koehr-tah-DOEHR DEE FEW

7) **rolo de pintura** (paint roller)
HOEH-loo DEE pin-TOO-rah

8) **motosserra** (chainsaw)
moeh-toeh-SEH-hah

9) **furadeira** (drill)
foo-rah-DAY-rah

10) **britadeira** (jackhammer)
bree-tah-DAY-rah

11) **alicate** (pliers)
ah-lee-KAH-chee

12) **chave de fenda** (screwdriver)
SHAH-vee DEE FEN-dah

A motosserra é muito barulhenta.
The chainsaw is too loud.

Eu preciso de um martelo para pendurar este quadro.
I need a hammer to hang this picture.

Me dê a chave de fenda.
Give me the screwdriver.

CONSTRUÇÃO II (CONSTRUCTION II)

1) **caixa de ferramentas** (toolbox)
   KAH-ee-shah DEE feah-hah-MEN-tahz

2) **capacete** (work helmet/hard hat)
   kah-pah-SEAH-chee

3) **planta** (blueprint)
   PLUN-tah

4) **canos** (pipes)
   KUH-nooz

5) **espátula** (trowel)
   es-PAH-too-lah

6) **misturador de concreto** (concrete mixer)
   meez-too-rah-DOEHR DEE kon-KREH-too

7) **tijolo** (brick)
   tee-ZHOEH-loo

8) **material de construção** (building materials)
   mah-taeh-ree-OW DEE kons-troo-SUH-oo

9) **azulejos** (tiles)
   ah-zhoo-LEAH-zhoos

10) **cimento** (cement)
    see-MEN-too

11) **areia** (sand)
    ah-RAY-ah

12) **cascalho** (gravel)
    kahz-KAH-llio

As casas inglesas são feitas de tijolos.
English houses are made of bricks.

Minha caixa de ferramentas está na garagem.
My toolbox is in the garage.

Nós colocamos cascalho em nosso jardim.
We have put gravel down in our front yard.

QUIZ #7

Use arrows to match the corresponding translations:

a. waitress

b. left

c. old

d. bus stop

e. wrong

f. playground

g. right

h. to talk

i. main course

j. closed

k. to sing

l. floor/story

m. to buy

n. to walk

o. inside

p. far

1. falar

2. andar

3. ver

4. cantar

5. direita

6. playground

7. piso

8. dentro

9. fechar

10. comprar

11. esquerda

12. errado

13. velho

14. garçonete

15. ponto de ônibus

16. prato principal

Fill in the blank spaces with the options below (use each word only once):

Aqui estão as instruções para chegar à _____. A partir da _____ no parque, _____ a primeira rua à _____ e continue até o _____. Quando a luz estiver verde, vire à esquerda. _____ da igreja há uma estação de _____. Passe a estação e _____ em frente por 10 minutos. A loja fica à esquerda.

semáforo   loja de roupas

ande   direita

fonte   pegue

atrás   metrô

PLANTAS E ÁRVORES (PLANTS AND TREES)

1) **flores silvestres** (wildflowers)
   FLOEH-reez sil-VEZ-treez

2) **erva** (herb)
   EHR-vah

3) **cogumelo** (mushroom)
   koeh-goo-MEH-loo

4) **erva daninha** (weed)
   EHR-vah duh-NEE-gnah

5) **algas** (seaweed)
   OW-gahz

6) **samambaia** (fern)
   sah-mum-BAH-ee-ah

7) **cana** (reed)
   KUH-nah

8) **bambu** (bamboo)
   bum-BOO

9) **hera** (ivy)
   EH-rah

10) **musgo** (moss)
    MOOZ-goo

11) **grama** (grass)
    GRUH-mah

12) **palmeira** (palm tree)
    pow-MAY-rah

13) **mangue** (mangrove)
    MUN-gee

14) **cacto** (cactus)
    KAHK-too

Ele me presenteou com um buquê de flores silvestres.
He gifted me a bouquet of wildflowers.

O bambu cresce rápido.
Bamboo grows very fast.

Hoje à noite comeremos macarrão com cogumelo.
Tonight, we are eating mushroom pasta.

159

O CARNAVAL (THE CARNIVAL)

1) **máscara** (mask)
MAHS-kah-rah

2) **fantasia** (costume)
fun-tah-ZEE-ah

3) **carro alegórico** (float)
KAH-hoo ah-leah-GAW-ree-koo

4) **flores** (flowers)
FLOEH-reez

5) **tarola** (snare drum)
tah-RAW-lah

6) **palhaço** (clown)
pah-LLIA-soo

7) **super-herói** (superhero)
SOO-peahr eah-RAW-ee

8) **princesa** (princess)
preen-SEAH-zah

9) **astronauta** (astronaut)
ahs-troeh-NOW-tah

10) **mímico** (mime)
MEE-mee-koo

11) **prisioneiro** (prisoner)
pree-zee-oeh-NAY-roo

12) **disfarce** (disguise)
deez-FAHR-see

13) **fada** (fairy)
FAH-dah

14) **lenhador** (lumberjack)
leah-gnah-DOEHR

Eu leio um conto de fadas para a minha filha todas as noites.
I read a fairy tale to my daughter every evening.

As pessoas usam máscaras no carnaval.
People wear masks during carnival.

Diana foi a princesa do povo.
Diana was the people's princess.

A OFICINA (THE WORKSHOP)

1) **ferramenta** (tool)
   feah-hah-MEN-tah

2) **selaria** (saddlery)
   seah-lah-REE-ah

3) **marcenaria** (carpentry/woodwork)
   mahr-seah-nah-REE-ah

4) **tapeçaria** (upholstery/tapestry)
   tah-peah-sah-REE-ah

5) **sapateiro** (shoemaking/shoe repair)
   sah-pah-TAY-roo

6) **ourives** (silversmith)
   o-REE-veez

7) **ferreiro** (blacksmith)
   feah-HAY-roo

8) **mecânico** (mechanic)
   meah-KUH-nee-koo

9) **têxtil** (textile)
   TEZ-till

10) **padaria** (bakery)
    pah-dah-REE-ah

11) **bijuterias feitas à mão** (handmade jewelry)
    bee-zhoo-teah-REE-as FAY-tahz AH MUH-oo

12) **calçados** (footwear)
    cow-SAH-dooz

13) **manutenção** (maintenance)
    mah-noo-ten-SUH-oo

14) **conserto** (repair)
    con-SEAHR-too

15) **pintura** (painting)
    pin-TOO-rah

16) **confeitaria** (pastry)
    kon-fay-tah-REE-ah

O mecânico terminou de consertar meu carro.
The mechanic has finished repairing my car.

Eu sou o técnico da manutenção.
I am the maintenance guy.

Eu gostaria de comprar sua pintura.
I would like to buy your painting.

O MERCADO (THE GROCERY STORE)

1) **macarrão** (pasta)
   mah-kah-HUH-oo

2) **arroz** (rice)
   ah-HOZ

3) **aveia** (oat)
   ah-VAY-ah

4) **pão** (bread)
   PUH-oo

5) **óleos** (oils)
   AW-llioz

6) **molhos** (sauces)
   MOEH-llioz

7) **molho de salada** (salad dressings)
   MOEH-llio DEE sah-LAH-dah

8) **temperos** (condiments)
   tem-PEAH-rooz

9) **enlatados** (canned goods)
   en-lah-TAH-dooz

10) **presunto** (ham)
    preah-ZOON-too

11) **queijo** (cheese)
    KAY-zhoo

12) **manteiga de amendoim** (peanut butter)
    mun-TAY-gah DEE ah-men-do-EEM

13) **doces** (candy)
    DOEH-sees

14) **feijão** (beans)
    fay-JUH-oo

15) **café** (coffee)
    kah-FEH

16) **chá** (tea)
    SHAH

Eu quero comer um sanduíche de manteiga de amendoim.
I want to eat a peanut butter sandwich.

Eu coloco leite de aveia no meu café.
I take oat milk in my coffee.

Você pode encontrar os melhores queijos do mundo na França.
You can find the best cheeses in the world in France.

VIAGEM E VIDA I (TRAVEL AND LIVING I)

1) **anfitrião** (host)
un-fee-tree-UH-oo

2) **turista** (tourist)
too-REEZ-tah

3) **viajante** (traveler)
vee-ah-ZHUN-chee

4) **bagagem** (luggage)
bah-GAH-zhem

5) **bagagem de mão** (hand luggage)
bah-GAH-zhem DEE MUH-oo

6) **câmera** (camera)
KUH-meah-rah

7) **hotel** (hotel)
oeh-TELL

8) **albergue** (hostal)
ahl-BEAR-ghee

9) **pousada** (Bed & Breakfast/inn)
po-ZAH-dah

10) **cabana** (cabin)
kah-BUH-nah

11) **barraca** (tent)
bah-HAH-kah

12) **voo** (flight)
VOEH-oo

13) **embarque** (departure)
em-BAHR-kee

14) **desembarque** (arrival)
deah-zem-BAHR-kee

Eu reservei uma pousada para três noites.
I booked a bed and breakfast for three nights.

O voo parte às 13:20h.
The flight departs at 1:30 p.m.

Não esqueça da câmera!
Do not forget the camera!

VIAGEM E VIDA II (TRAVEL AND LIVING II)

1) **cidade** (town)
see-DAH-dee

2) **mapa** (map)
MAH-pah

3) **ponto de ônibus** (bus stop)
PON-too DEE OEH-nee-booz

4) **táxi** (taxi)
TAHK-see

5) **locadora de carros** (car rental)
loeh-kah-DOEH-rah DEE KAH-hoos

6) **estação de trem** (train station)
ez-tah-SUH-oo DEE TREM

7) **aeroporto** (airport)
ah-eah-roeh-POHR-too

8) **passaporte** (passport)
pah-sah-POHR-chee

9) **identidade** (ID/identification card)
ee-den-chee-DAH-dee

10) **moeda** (currency)
moe-EH-dah

11) **dinheiro** (cash)
dee-GNAY-roo

12) **cartão de débito** (debit card)
kahr-TUH-oo DEE DEH-bee-too

13) **cartão de crédito** (credit card)
kahr-TUH-oo DEE KREH-dee-too

14) **guia turístico** (tourist guide)
GEE-ah too-REEZ-chee-koo

Eu tenho que renovar meu passaporte.
I must renew my passport.

Você vai pagar no cartão de débito ou em dinheiro?
Are you paying by debit card or cash?

Você pode reservar um táxi para mim?
Could you book a taxi for me?

BRINQUEDOS (TOYS)

1) **bola** (ball)
   BOH-lah

2) **urso de pelúcia** (teddy bear)
   OOHR-soo DEE peah-LOO-see-ah

3) **trem** (train)
   TREHM

4) **skate** (skateboard)
   ez-KAY-chee

5) **boneca** (doll)
   boeh-NEH-kah

6) **carrinho de corrida** (race car)
   kah-HEE-gnoo DEE koeh-HEE-dah

7) **robô** (robot)
   hoe-BOE

8) **pipa** (kite)
   PEE-pah

9) **bateria** (drums)
   bah-teah-REE-ah

10) **bambolê** (hula hoop)
    bum-boeh-LEAH

11) **carrinho** (wagon)
    kah-HEE-gnoo

12) **blocos** (blocks)
    BLOH-kooz

13) **xilofone** (xylophone)
    shee-loeh-FOEH-nee

14) **caminhão** (truck)
    kah-mee-GNUH-oo

15) **avião** (airplane)
    ah-vee-UH-oo

16) **tijolos** (bricks)
    chee-ZHOEH-looz

Eu aprendi a tocar bateria dez anos atrás.
I learned to play the drums 10 years ago.

Minha filha perdeu seu urso de pelúcia.
My daughter has lost her teddy bear.

Joga a bola para mim!
Throw me the ball!

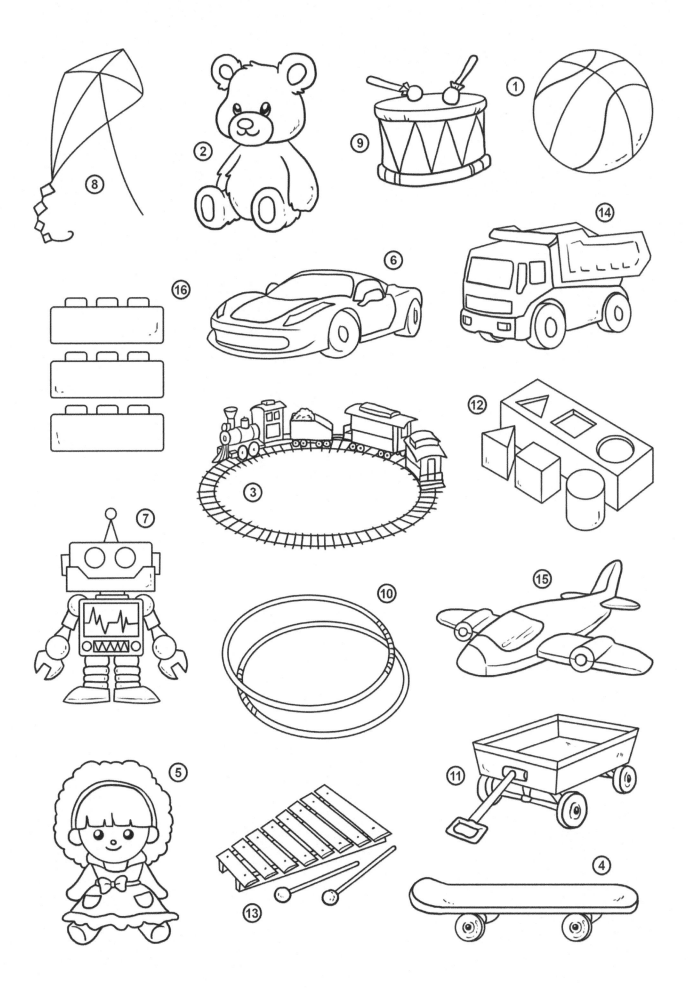

A FESTA DE ANIVERSÁRIO (THE BIRTHDAY PARTY)

1) **faixa de aniversário** (birthday banner)
FAH-ee-shah DEE ah-nee-vehr-SAH-ree-oo

2) **decoração** (decoration)
deah-coeh-rah-SUH-oo

3) **presente** (present/gift)
preah-ZEN-chee

4) **toalha** (tableware)
toeh-AH-lliah

5) **aniversariante** (birthday person)
ah-nee-vehr-sah-ree-UN-chee

6) **balão** (balloon)
bah-LUH-oo

7) **bolo de aniversário** (birthday cake)
BOEH-loo DEE ah-nee-vehr-SAH-ree-oo

8) **pratos** (plates)
PRAH-toos

9) **garfos** (forks)
GAHR-fooz

10) **colheres** (spoons)
koeh-LLIE-reez

11) **copos** (cups)
KOH-pooz

12) **canudo** (straw)
kah-NOO-doo

13) **pinhata** (piñata)
pee-GNAH-tah

14) **vela** (candle)
VEH-lah

15) **chapéu** (hat)
shah-PELL

16) **convidados** (guests)
con-vee-DAH-doos

Eu recebi muitos presentes no meu aniversário.
I received a lot of gifts for my birthday.

Todos os convidados foram embora.
All the guests have left.

Ela fez um arco de balões para mim.
She made me a balloon arch.

OPOSTOS (OPPOSITES)

1) **limpo/a** (clean)
LEEM-poo/pah

2) **sujo/a** (dirty)
SOO-zhoo/zhah

3) **poucos/as** (few)
PO-koehz/kahz

4) **muitos/as** (many)
MOO-ee-tooz/tahz

5) **ataque** (attack)
ah-TAH-kee

6) **defesa** (defense)
deah-FEAH-zah

7) **reto** (straight)
REH-too

8) **curvo/a** (curved)
KOOHR-voo/vah

9) **juntos/as** (together)
ZHOON-tooz/tahz

10) **separados/as** (separated)
se-pah-RAH-dooz/dahz

11) **jovem** (young)
ZHAW-vem

12) **velho/a** (old)
VEH-llio/llia

13) **riqueza** (wealth)
hee-KEAH-zah

14) **escassez** (shortage)
ez-kah-CEZ

15) **côncavo/a** (concave)
KON-kah-voo/vah

16) **convexo/a** (convex)
kon-VEHK-soo/sah

Meus pais são separados.
My parents are separated.

Eu sou o mais novo.
I am the youngest.

Este prato está sujo.
This plate is dirty.

QUIZ #8

Use arrows to match the corresponding translations:

a. arrival

b. cheese

c. cups

d. tourist guide

e. map

f. forks

g. town

h. candle

i. doll

j. airport

k. truck

l. flowers

m. few

n. traveler

o. rice

p. candy

1. poucos

2. boneca

3. flores

4. caminhão

5. viajante

6. queijo

7. doce

8. aeroporto

9. arroz

10. cidade

11. xícaras

12. mapa

13. desembarque

14. vela

15. guia de turismo

16. garfos

Fill in the blank spaces with the options below (use each word only once):

Minha prima Sofia veio me visitar no meu aniversário. A viagem dela foi horrível. Para começar, o _____ para levá-la ao _____ não apareceu. Ela quase perdeu seu _____. Quando ela desceu do avião, percebeu que havia deixado sua _____, que continha sua carteira junto com seu _____ e sua _____, no aeroporto. Quando ela chegou à _____, havia tantos _____ que todas as ruas estavam bloqueadas com engarrafamentos. Ela queria parar e comprar um _____, mas não conseguiu encontrar uma padaria porque também tinha perdido seu _____. Ela também não tinha um presente, então parou na única loja que ainda estava aberta, uma loja de brinquedos, e comprou um _____ muito fofo.

turistas

identidade

cidade

aeroporto

passaporte

táxi

bolo de aniversário

voo

mapa

bagagem de mão

urso de pelúcia

CONCLUSION

While there is much more to say about the Portuguese language, we hope that this general overview will help you understand and use the words and phrases in this dictionary, as well as your own words and phrases, as you continue your journey to bilingualism.

We would like to leave you with a few suggestions for a pleasant and fruitful language learning experience:

1. Learn what you need and what you love.

   While survival Portuguese is indispensable, mechanical memorization of long lists of words is not the best use of your time and energy. Make sure to focus on the vocabulary that is important and useful to you in your life. Perhaps you need Portuguese for work, or to visit family and friends. In this case, make sure you focus on the vocabulary that will be useful to reach these goals.

2. Do not skip learning grammar and tenses. Although it is not always the most exciting part of learning a language, spending some time perfecting your grammar is the key to being able to master your language skills in the long term.

3. Use available media to practice all aspects of the language. Movies, music, and social media provide the opportunity to practice reading, writing, and listening at any time from your phone or your computer. Aim to spend 20 minutes a day practicing Portuguese to make good progress.

4. Practice speaking with a native speaker as soon as you can. You can join speaking groups in real life or online.

5. Remember: **Communication before perfection**. It takes years to master a language, and fluency is not achieved easily. It requires commitment and regular practice. However, if you get the opportunity to visit a Portuguese-speaking country, do not hesitate to try to speak Portuguese to everyone you meet. This will give you the motivation and the confidence to carry on learning. You might feel scared at first, but do not worry; people will be kind to you!

6. Enjoy the journey!

ANSWERS

QUIZ #1

a-13.   b-11.   c-10.   d-15.   e-9.   f-12.   g-6.   h-14.   i-8.   j-1.   k-5.   l-2.
m-16.   n-7.   o-4.   p-3.

Minha **mãe** e meu pai estão separados há anos. Todo mundo fica **surpreso** com o quanto eles se dão bem para um **casal divorciado**. Minha **irmã** é minha melhor amiga. Ela é **bondosa** e tem um **coração** de ouro. Eu sou **séria,** e todo mundo diz que tenho muita **coragem**. Eu gosto de animais, especialmente **cachorros**. Fomos convidados para jantar na casa do meu pai amanhã à noite. Eu acho que ele vai preparar um **peru**. Eu espero estar me sentindo melhor, porque hoje minha **cabeça** dói e meu nariz está **entupido**.

QUIZ # 2

a-10.   b-5.   c-8.   d-9.   e-2.   f-13.   g-15.   h-16.   i-3.   J-12.   k-1.   l-4.
m-6.   n-7.   o-11.   p-14.

Lisa é professora de jardim de infância. Na semana passada, ela levou a turma para uma fazenda. A previsão dizia que ia chover, mas estava muito **calor**. O dia inteiro foi **ensolarado**. Lisa vestiu **calças**, **sapatos** e um grande **casaco**. Infelizmente, ela se sentiu desconfortável o dia inteiro. Durante a visita à fazenda, as crianças viram porcos, cavalos e **vacas**. Havia também uma colmeia com centenas de **abelhas**. Também havia **vespas,** e uma delas picou a Lisa!

QUIZ # 3

a-16.   b-14.   c-9.   d-8.   e-7.   f-11.   G-3.   h-5.   i-13.   j-12.   k-4.   l-2.
m-1.   n-15.   o-6   p-10.

O outono é a minha estação favorita. Todos os anos, aguardo com impaciência o mês de outubro, porque decoro o **jardim**. Eu também decoro minha **sacada**. Meus amigos e eu gostamos de esculpir **abóboras** e colocá-las por toda a casa. Eu sempre coloco uma na frente da **lareira**; elas parecem **lâmpadas** assustadoras! 31 de outubro é o Halloween. Nesta data, vamos até a casa dos vizinhos para pegar doces. Então, por volta da **meia-noite**, acendemos **velas aromatizadas** e relaxamos no **banco** com **chocolate quente**. Às vezes, também jogamos no console de **videogame**. Em novembro, eu vou **esquiar** na **pista de gelo** da cidade. Estou animado!

QUIZ # 4

a-15.　b-7.　c-9.　d-13.　e-11.　f-10.　g-12.　h-14.　i-8.　J-2.　k-1.　l-16.
m-4.　n-5.　o-6.　p-3.

Pedro é **aluno** de Engenharia Civil na Universidade de Delft. Ele está no terceiro ano. No futuro, ele quer ser **engenheiro** ou **empresário**. Seu objetivo é ficar rico e viajar pelo mundo. Ele sonha em jogar **vôlei** em uma **praia** no Caribe. Ele também sonha em sair na água com seu próprio **barco** ou com um **jet ski**. Seu **professor** favorito é o Sr. Silva. Ele é muito inteligente e carismático. Pedro gostaria de seguir seus passos. No entanto, agora ele tem que ir à lavanderia para usar a **máquina de lavar** e lavar a **roupa suja**. Para isso, ele deve primeiro ir ao supermercado comprar **sabão** e **amaciante de roupas**.

QUIZ # 5

a-7.　b-3.　c-15　d-13.　e-12.　f-11.　g-2.　h-16.　i-14.　j-8.　k-6.　l-4.
m-5.　n-1.　o-10.　p-9.

Meus avós moram na **América do Sul**, no **norte** do Brasil. Eu decidi visitá-los no próximo mês. Não nos vemos com muita frequência porque moro em Nova York, mas graças ao meu **computador** e **webcam**, mantemos contato. Minha avó é uma excelente tocadora de **piano**. Ela costumava tocar em bares da cidade. Ela me ensinou a tocar **guitarra elétrica**! Meu avô é **fazendeiro**. Ele planta **repolho**. Ele faz os bolos mais deliciosos do mundo com **morangos** e **framboesa**.

QUIZ # 6

a-11.　b-7.　c-9.　d-2.　e-15.　f-14.　g-12.　h-13.　i-16.　j-6.　k-1.　l-8.
m-3.　n-4.　o-5.　p-10.

Paula e suas amigas fizeram um delicioso jantar para comemorar o **aniversário** de Joana. Em setembro, todas elas vão **começar a universidade**. Paula só vai estudar no ano que vem, porque ela quer **viajar o mundo primeiro**. A comida não era **barata**, mas o jantar valeu a pena. Estava uma delícia. Como aperitivo havia **vieiras** e **caranguejo**. Pauline ficou feliz porque gosta de frutos do mar. Depois veio o prato principal. Elas poderiam escolher entre **lasanha** e **frango** com **batata**. Pauline optou pelo frango, mas infelizmente estava **duro** e um pouco queimado, e as demais acharam a lasanha com muito **sal**. Como **sobremesa**, elas desfrutaram de um delicioso fondant de chocolate.

QUIZ # 7

a-14. b-11. c-13. d-15. e-12. f-6. g-5. h-1. i-16. j-9. k-4. l-7.
m-10. n-2. o-8. p-3.

Aqui estão as instruções para chegar à **loja de roupas**. A partir da **fonte** no parque, **pegue** a primeira rua à **direita** e continue até o **semáforo**. Quando a luz estiver verde, vire à esquerda. **Atrás** da igreja há uma estação de **metrô**. Passe a estação e **ande** em frente por 10 minutos. A loja fica à esquerda.

QUIZ # 8

a-13. b-6. c-11. d-15. e-12. f-16. g-10. h-14. i-2. j-8. k-4. l-3.
m-1. n-5. o-9. p-7.

Minha prima Sofia veio me visitar no meu aniversário. A viagem dela foi horrível. Para começar, o **táxi** para levá-la ao **aeroporto** não apareceu. Ela quase perdeu seu **voo**. Quando ela desceu do avião, percebeu que havia deixado sua **bagagem de mão**, que continha sua carteira junto com seu **passaporte** e sua **identidade, no aeroporto**. Quando ela chegou à **cidade**, havia tantos **turistas** que todas as ruas estavam bloqueadas com engarrafamentos. Ela queria parar e comprar um **bolo de aniversário**, mas não conseguiu encontrar uma padaria porque também tinha perdido seu **mapa**. Ela também não tinha um presente, então parou na única loja que ainda estava aberta, uma loja de brinquedos, e comprou um **urso de pelúcia** muito fofo.

Made in the USA
Las Vegas, NV
01 December 2022

60696408R00105